PURNELL LIBRARY OF KNOWLEDGE
Rockets and How They Work

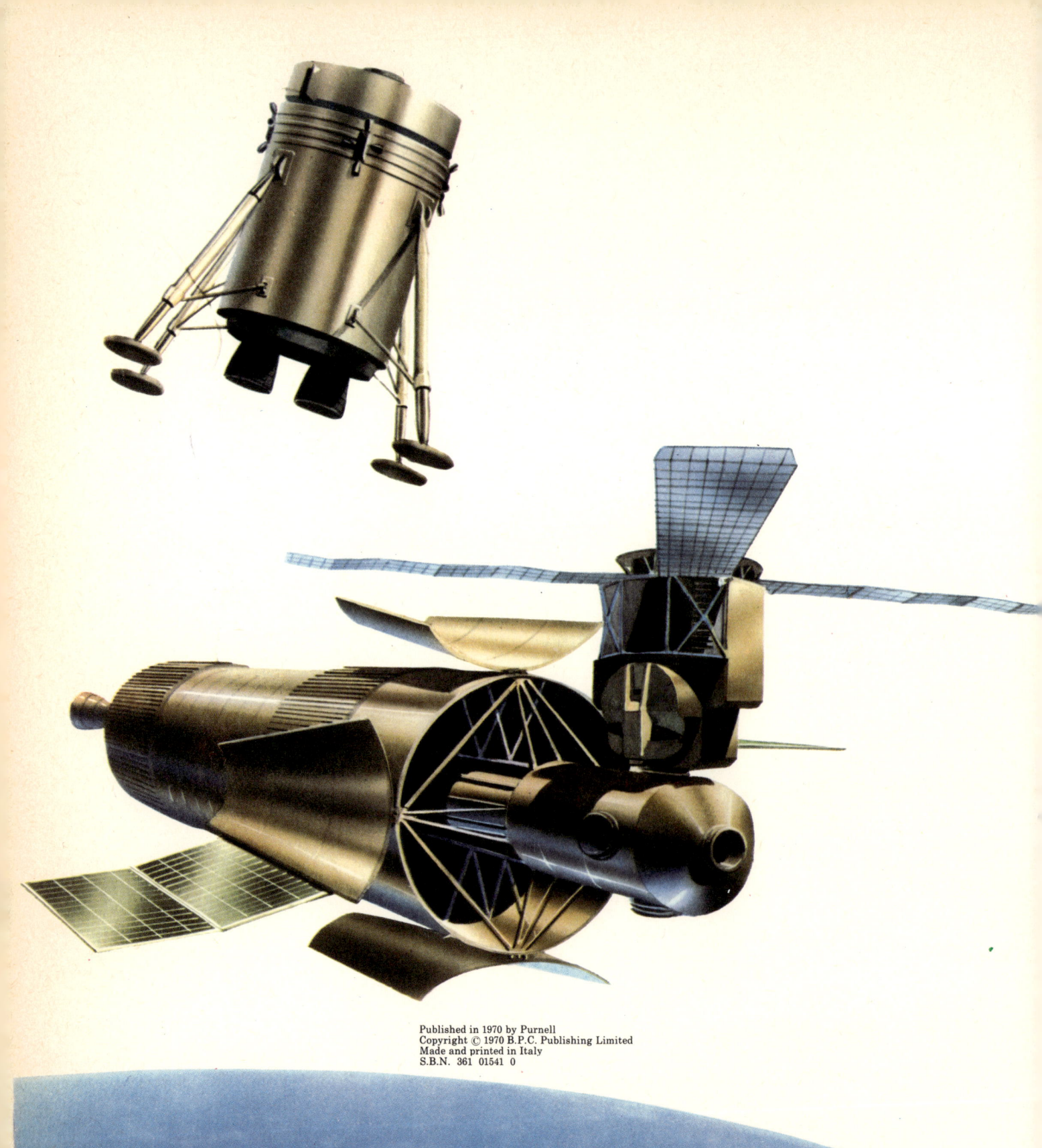

Published in 1970 by Purnell
Copyright © 1970 B.P.C. Publishing Limited
Made and printed in Italy
S.B.N. 361 01541 0

Rockets and How They Work

By Frank Farr
Illustrated by
Eric Eden

PURNELL

London

Introduction

The story of rockets is an important and exciting part of man's continual quest for knowledge. Since man first discovered fire and its uses and the Chinese first invented "fire arrows", the science of rocketry has been concerned with the whole of mankind's progress.

The author has presented the background and the facts about rocket technology beginning with the earliest rocket weapons. Here, too, are the attempts in the early part of the twentieth century by the great rocket pioneers — the Russian mathematician Konstantin Tsiolkowsky, the American scientist Robert Goddard, and the German scientist Hermann Oberth – to make missiles that could be propelled through the air. The failures and the magnificent triumphs of modern rocketry—missiles, satellites and spacecraft—are described in simple, brief sections illustrated with detailed drawings and diagrams in colour and black and white.

The rocket has come a long way in its development—from firework, signal flare, lifeline-thrower and weapon of war to sophisticated space traveller. For rockets are the only means of propulsion known that work effectively in airless space. The short history of man's journeys into space and his dependence upon the rocket for transport, not only to the Moon but beyond in our Solar System and perhaps to other Galaxies, profoundly affects our lives today and tomorrow. It is the rocket that propels man into a future that is more than just thrilling science fiction speculation.

Contents

Chapter 1 Beginnings	12
Congreve	14
Steps in the Right Direction	16
Misplaced Enthusiasm	18
Prophets	20
Chapter 2 How a Rocket Works	22
Liquid and Solid Fuels	22
Guidance	24
Performance	26
Speed	28
Steering and Stability	30
Chapter 3 What Rockets Do	32
Sounding Rockets	32
The Beginning of the Big Ones	34
Work Horses	36
Atlas	38
Rocket Planes	40
Lifting Off	44
Rocket Pilots	46
Space Stations	48
The Sputniks	50
Mariner Space Probes	52
Mariner 4	54
Titan, Delta, Agena	56
The Mercury Project	58
Russian Cosmonauts	60
Gemini	62
Getting the Message	64
Space Probe – Moon	66
Saturn I	68
Saturn V	70
The Apollo Programme	72
Launching Sites	76
The Back – Up	78
Nuclear Rockets	80
Cancelled	82
The Rocket Industry	84
Odd-Ideas	86
Electric Systems	88
On to the Stars	90
Index	92

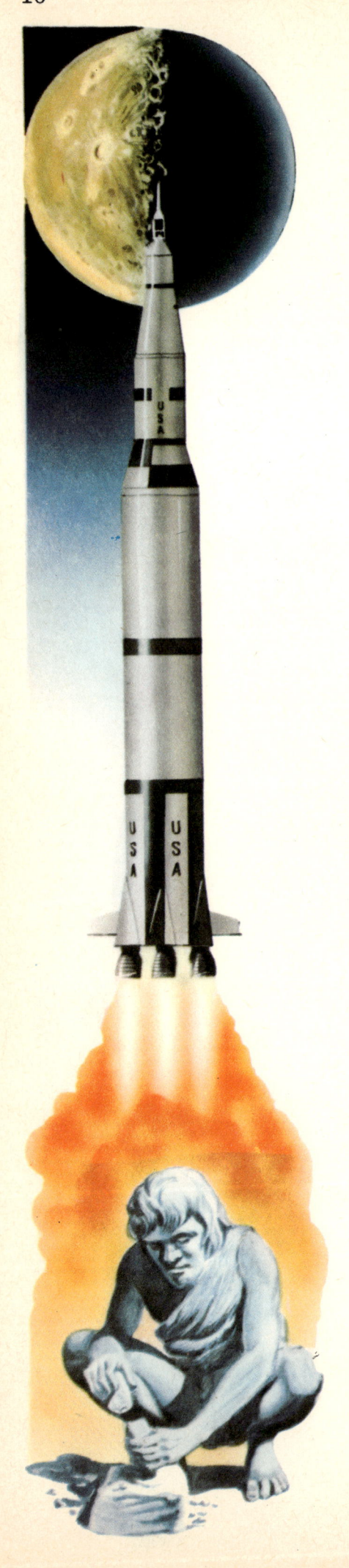

Background

During the last dozen or so years there has been a tremendous increase in the size and scope of rockets, and newspaper headlines have repeatedly heralded The Dawn of the Space-Age. Great strides have also been taken in many other scientific fields. We are said to be living in the Nuclear Age, the Genetic Age, the Radio Astronomy Age – to name but three alternatives – and are witnessing, to quote the title of a book by Sir Bernard Lovell, 'The Explosion in Science'.

If science is 'organised curiosity', it is this disciplined inquisitiveness that distinguishes Man from his fellow creatures. Animal curiosity is generally at the level of the blue tit's peck at a milk bottle top, but Man's curiosity takes him far beyond a quest for food, and it has rewarded him well. There have always been men who wanted to know 'What would happen if . . . ?' – and the answers they found have frequently been put to many different uses. The rocket, for example, has been in its time a a weapon of war, a firework, a signal flare and a lifeline thrower; now it is being used as the only means of propulsion that works more efficiently in airless space than it does in the atmosphere.

This means of propulsion of modern spacecraft could not have existed without prior discoveries in metallurgy, chemistry, mathematics, electricity – the list is endless. In the distant beginnings of rocketry, when technology as we know it was undreamt of, simple tools must have been used to construct the first 'fire arrows', and the family tree of tools goes right back to the first sharpened stone chipped by primitive man in prehistoric times.

Rocket research, then, does not exist as the isolated concern of a few scientists, technicians and test pilots; it is an inseparable part of the whole of Man's quest for knowledge.

What practical benefits may we expect from Space research? There are thousands of items that owe their initial production to space flight, and, given the current tempo of space research, there will undoubtedly soon be thousands more. Perhaps the new standards of precision and perfection that have been developed within the specialised production of space machinery will spill over into other industries. The aircraft industry should certainly benefit. To satisfy the stringent demands of astronautics, many products have been highly developed. The fuel cell, for example – a means of producing electricity without cumbersome generating plant – provides power in spacecraft and may soon perform the same service for homes and electric vehicles. Already lighter batteries, improved cooking utensils, micro-miniature electronic components, fireproof paints, new flexible pipes for fluids and new plastics are coming into service. Satellites are another important development of space research. In addition to gathering information for scientists, they provide television and telephone relays, aid navigation of ships and aircraft, and provide useful data about the exact shape of the world and its geology.

All this is a far cry from the the rocket's early beginnings. As the heading panels in strip cartoon stories have it, this is 'The story so far... Now read on...'

The famous **Sputnik 1** *– the Russian satellite which was successfully launched on October 4th 1957 was surprisingly big and heavy. It weighed 184 lbs and had a diameter of 23 inches*

Beginnings

Imagine a world without modern innovations, where cooking was done on a wood fire, travel was by horseback or on foot, and weapons were confined to the sword and spear. It was in these conditions that gunpowder was discovered.

Perhaps, however, the discovery was not so strange after all. Gunpowder is a mixture of charcoal, saltpetre and sulphur – all of which would have been familiar substances to the discoverer. Charcoal would have been used by metalsmiths, rather like barbecue cooks use it today, for its property of producing a clear bright flame and giving off much heat. Saltpetre, found in places where nitrogenous matter has decayed, is a white, crystalline substance. One can imagine old straw from a stable used as tinder for firelighting, and it being noticed that the stalks with white salt-like stuff adhering to them burnt with a fiercer blaze. Sulphur occurs naturally, especially in volcanic regions. Perhaps the inventor was trying to make some sort of firebomb to lob at enemies. If so, he must have had a surprise when its explosive nature became apparent.

Eventually someone conceived the notion of putting this powder mixture inside an open-ended tube before lighting it – and the rocket was born.

Fire arrows and today's ballistic missiles are alike in that they both burn explosive fuels – fuels that burn very rapidly, producing gas. We see this

Early in the thirteenth century the Chinese used "arrows of fire" against the attacking hordes of the all-conquering Monguls. Knowledge of the "arrow" rocket later spread westward. By the end of the century rockets were being used in European battles

An explosion which occurs during burning when the chemicals combine violently and give off a large quantity of gas at a very high temperature. The explosion is contained within the simple tube-like shape of a rocket and operates on the closed end of the tube thereby propelling the rocket forwards

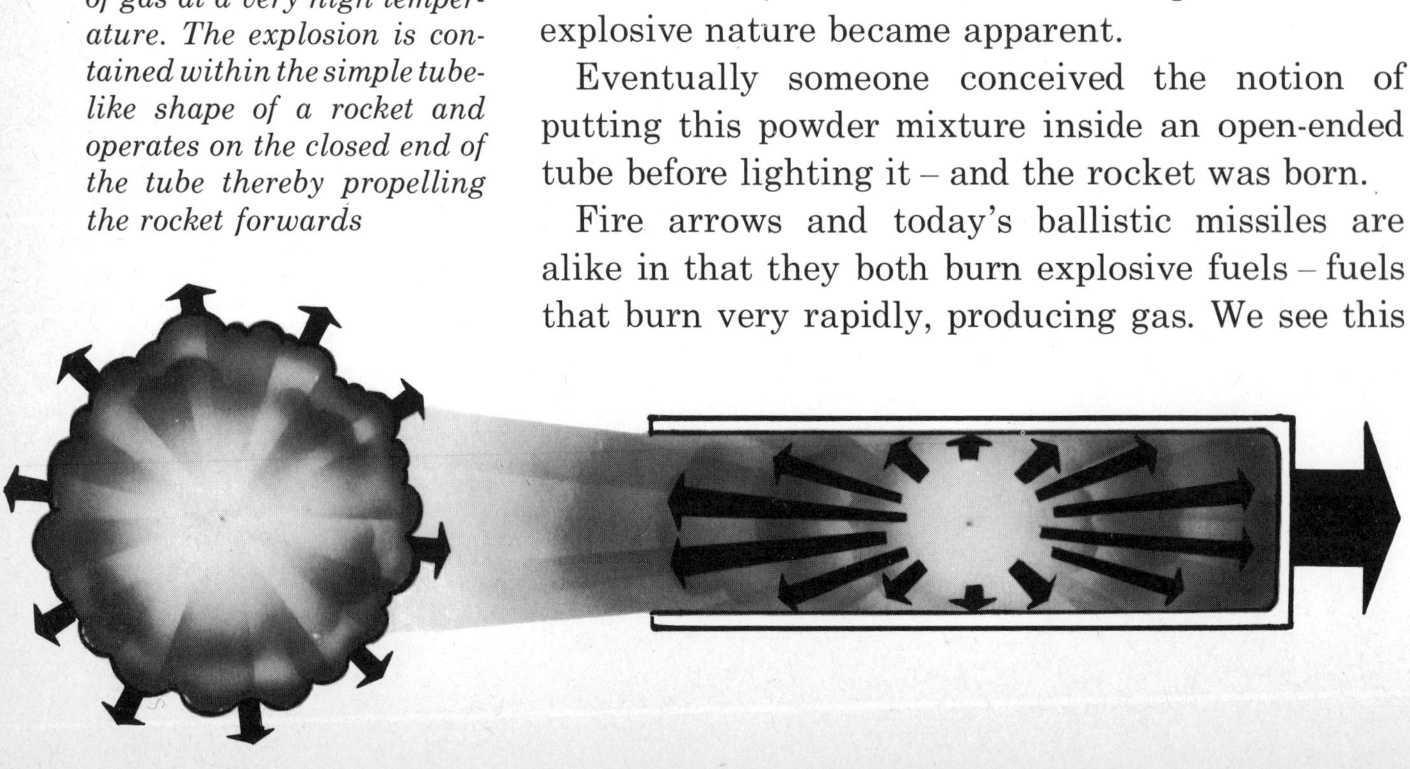

in the flame of a rocket's exhaust. In the case of the fire arrow, the charcoal and sulphur burn fiercely in the oxygen released by the heated saltpetre, producing carbon and sulphur dioxide gases in large amounts.

These expanding gases provide the thrust that propels the rocket. The power is controlled by the shape and size of the thrust chamber where the explosion occurs, and the nozzle which accelerates and directs the flow of gas.

Following on its Chinese origin, knowledge of the rocket and its fuel spread westward by way of India, Arabia, Greece and Byzantium. By the end of the thirteenth century rockets were being used in European battles. Not long afterwards a new weapon appeared – the cannon. At first primitive and unreliable, these guns were eventually improved until they could be aimed with more accuracy than rockets, and the rocket then began to fall from favour. (It is significant that the explosive is called gunpowder, although the mixture was first used to propel rockets.) However, as rockets were much easier and cheaper to make than guns, and could be easily transported into battle, their use persisted, especially when it was possible to set fire to enemy fortifications. Fifteenth-century pirates still found them useful for setting light to their victims' ships, but by the sixteenth century rockets had been relegated to the peaceful role of providing firework displays.

Constructing a firework rocket: A paper tube is placed over a tapering spindle and charged with powder. When full, the spindle is withdrawn, leaving a narrow, conical hole – the burning cavity. Below this the tube is pinched in to form a nozzle. The explosive head is separated from the charge itself by a clay plug. A fuse or quick match carries the flame to the bursting charge, when the fuel is exhausted, through a small hole in the plug, and the rocket stars explode

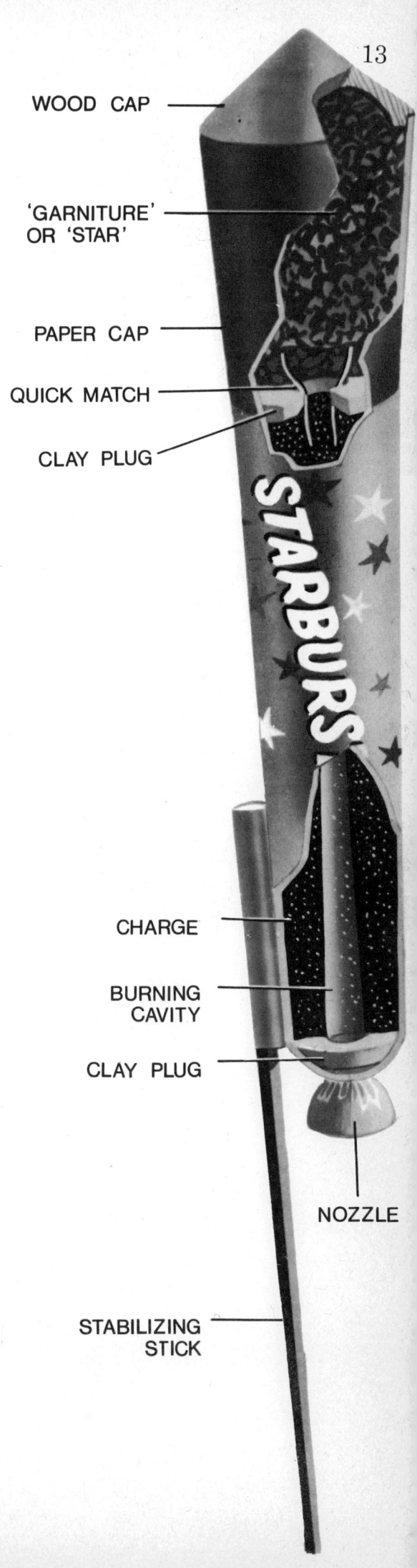

Congreve

Rocket research, then, does not exist as the English ships, trails of fire rose in fiery arcs that swept across the night sky, over the masts of the vessels in the harbour, then down among the buildings of the seaport town. The rockets rose and fell in their hundreds and, inside an hour, the town was ablaze.

This was not D-Day, 1944, but an assault on Boulogne in 1806, using Congreve rockets. The attack was directed against the shipping in the harbour, but the wind carried the missiles over their target. Encouraged by the destruction of an enemy town, William Congreve decided to develop a weapon to harass the forces of Napoleon. The following year, 25,000 rockets inflicted great damage on Copenhagen, and a rocket brigade took part in the battle of Waterloo. Soon afterwards, almost every European country had its rocket squads.

All this sprang from the experiments of William Congreve at the beginning of the nineteenth century. As the son of the Royal Laboratory Comptroller, he was able to make use of facilities at the Royal Arsenal and to bring his demonstration models before the authorities. He could also draw

18th century rockets. The cylindrical one carried an incendiary head which embedded a pointed nose in the target and then oozed a slow burning mixture of saltpetre, sulphur, antimony sulphide, tallow rosin and turpentine. The spherical rocket carried an explosive pay load which ejected case shot on its final explosion

on the knowledge of the firework makers who preceded him, and, as an educated man, he was undoubtedly familiar with Newton's third law of motion, which clearly defines the theory of rocket movement.

Some years before Congreve began 'souping up' firework rockets there had been an action in India in which British troops were bombarded with rockets by the soldiers of the Maharajah of Mysore. These missiles, which had cases less than a foot in length and diameters of a couple of inches, were attached to a ten-foot bamboo pole, and had a range of 1,000 yards. After his experiments had borne fruit, Congreve's rockets measured twice the size and travelled three times as far as the Indian rockets, although, as can be seen from the Boulogne episode, wind could upset their accuracy. In fact, it was not unknown for the missile to be swung round in flight in gusty weather so that it dived on its launchers. As the warheads were either explosive or incendiary, this was highly disconcerting.

To increase the range of his rockets, Congreve used a more violent powder than the skyrocket mixture. Had there been air spaces left between the granules, the charge would have exploded with enough violence to burst the stout iron case. To prevent this, the charge was first damped with alcohol before being rammed into the rocket. This dangerous operation was performed with the case immersed in water to reduce the risk.

All in all, Congreve improved the powder rocket as much as was possible with the knowledge available. His rockets were powerful and destructive (among papers found after his death were notes on a thousand-pounder!), but accuracy was not their strong point. Latterly he made the cases with an inward slope to the back. The guide stick could not be mounted on the side, so it was screwed into a plate on the bottom of the rocket. This plate had five small nozzles grouped round the stick insertion. The central stick improved the accuracy and, for a time, rockets could be fired straighter and farther than the guns of the period could shoot their shells.

19th century rocket maker William Congreve experimented with various designs to improve accuracy. Some rockets he made had an inward slope to the back and the guide stick was screwed into a plate on the bottom of the rocket. Others had centre sticks, fins and step concepts

Steps in the Right Direction

William Hale used the principle of the windmill to make rockets spin as they travelled. This idea is called spin stabilization and is used today on some small missiles

Soon after Congreve's death it began to look as though war rockets had been rendered obsolete by vastly improved guns. Spiral grooves or 'rifling' on the inside of the gun barrels caused the shells fired from them to emerge from the barrels with an imparted spin that kept them on a steady course. Rocket makers sought ways to make their missiles spin too. An Englishman, William Hale, thought of mounting canted vanes in the rocket's exhaust. The gas passing over these vanes turned them as wind turns a windmill; and, as the vanes were fixed to the outer case, the whole rocket thereby rotated. Spin stabilization, as this is called, is still used today on some smaller missiles, but its application to rockets in the nineteenth century did not save them from being pushed into temporary oblivion – with one small exception – until World War II. The exception was the French use of rockets against the Zeppelins in World War I. These hydrogen-filled airships were an obvious target for incendiary missiles, and a sitting duck for the Nieuport Scout, a fighter plane, equipped with a battery of eight rockets, four to each wing.

Meanwhile, the rocket was being used with considerable success in another sphere. In the early part of the nineteenth century the steamship was in its infancy; sailing craft were the principal ocean-going vessels. In gale conditions, modern steam vessels are sometimes driven ashore; for wind-driven sailing ships, this was an even greater hazard. One of the vessels which met its end in this way was the frigate *Anson*, whose crew perished with only sixty feet of turbulent water between them and safety. A Cornish cabinet-maker, Henry Trengrouse, witnessed the disaster and afterwards tried to think of ways in which a rescue might have been carried out. The result of his deliberations was the first life-saving rocket.

Others had a hand in later developments, but the

most successful rocket was devised by an artillery officer, Colonel Boxer. Like its predecessors, his rocket was designed to carry a thin line to a stricken ship, so that the crew could use it to pull a rope aboard on which a breeches buoy could carry them to safety. This kind of device is still in use today. They are also carried by ships, and lifeboats use a pistol-fired version.

Colonel Boxer's rocket was more successful because it was more powerful, using the principle of a step-rocket – or one mounted on another. This idea was not new; firework makers had experimented with step, or multi-stage, rockets since the sixteenth century. Boxer's step rockets could fly far enough and high enough to drop a line over a sinking ship.

Ship rescue is not the only use to which rockets have been put, apart from missiles and space vehicles. They can be used as signal flares, and once, in the early 1930s, they were used by an Austrian inventor to deliver mail in mountainous regions. A mailbag was fired by rocket and then made a parachute descent as the rocket fell.

The **Nieuport Scout** a World War I fighter plane which carried eight rockets. The rockets were used against hydrogen-filled airships

Misplaced Enthusiasm

Rocket power has also been applied to land and air vehicles. One set of experiments that drew public interest in 1928 was that conducted by Fritz von Opel, a German car manufacturer. During this period a group of enthusiasts in Germany had formed a rocket society which they called 'Verein für Raumschiffahrt', or Society for Space Travel. Their only hope of finance was the possibility of donations from members of the public. One of their number, Max Valier, managed to persuade von Opel to foot the bill for the building of a rocket-propelled car. Eventually Valier succeeded in building one that attained a modest 55 m.p.h., but this was sufficient to encourage von Opel to proceed with another, getting his own engineers to attach 12 rockets to the back of a racing car from which the engine had been removed. In this car, which Opel called the Opel Rak 1 (Rak being short for Raketen, or rockets) a speed of 70 m.p.h. was attained. Thus encouraged, Herr Opel then built a 'special' – the Opel Rak 2 which reached 125 m.p.h. To put these figures into historical perspective, it should be noted that in 1927 car races were being won at speeds of up to 100 m.p.h. and the land-speed record over a measured mile was held by Henry Seagrave with a speed of 200 m.p.h.

The Opel Rak achievement was sufficient to set off a minor wave of enthusiasm for this daring new mode of transport. Probably the least enthusiastic were the members of the Space Travel Society, for they knew that the rocket is out of its element in

The **Opel Rak 2,** a rocket propelled car which reached a speed of 125 m.p.h.

Another of Herr Opel's inventions – a rocket propelled glider

atmosphere, and is most efficient only when its speed approaches that of its exhaust, and such speed is far in excess of anything that is practical on land.

The members of the German rocket society were not only displeased with Valier for initiating land use of rockets; they were also unhappy about the publicity given to solid-fuel rockets when they themselves were struggling to raise funds to finance experiments with liquid-fuel propulsion. Their sights were fixed on the planets and beyond, and they knew that to overcome Earth's gravity pull they would need a speed of 25,000 m.p.h.; the only chemicals with sufficient exhaust velocity to propel a rocket at this speed were liquids, or gases in liquid forms; therefore the design of a rocket which would burn such fuel was the all-important first step.

Valier next embarked on a project for a car propelled by liquid-fuel rockets, which somewhat mollified the rocket society members. Unfortunately Valier was killed when his new motor exploded, and the tragedy caused a public demand for the cessation of rocket experimentation.

Max Valier's rocket propelled car only reached a speed of 55 m.p.h.

Prophets

One of the fathers of modern space-flight, Konstantin Tsiolkowsy was one of the first men to design a rocket for living in. Amongst his other ideas were passenger capsules with triple skins to protect the occupants from atmospheric friction-heat, methods for purifying the air inside the capsules, and igniting the motors and launching the spaceship by rocket-propelled sledge. He also conceived the step rocket or rocket train.

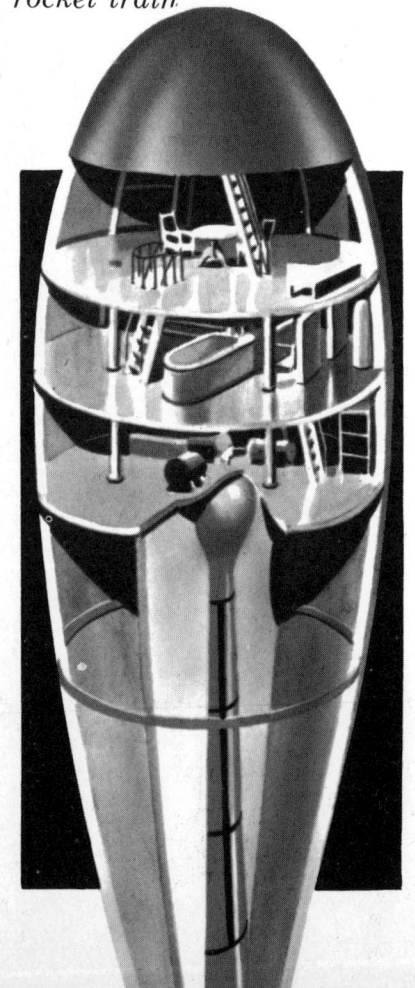

Though saddened by Valier's death, the German Space Travel enthusiasts could not rest until a liquid-fuel rocket had been made to work.

Down the ages men have dreamed of voyaging to the moon and planets. The first suggestions were, in the light of present knowledge, nothing less than fantastic. They ranged from sailing ships to contraptions supplied with multi-swan-power lift. Possibly the nearest to the ideas of the twentieth century was the invention of a fourteenth-century Chinese, Wan Hu. He sat in an armchair to which were attached fortyseven rockets. All the fuses were lit at once and Wan Hu disappeared in a cloud of flame and smoke – though not, alas, to the moon. More recently Jules Verne wrote a story of a trip to the moon in a series of novels about fictitious journeys. In contrast to what had gone before, Verne's stories were made credible by attention to scientific detail. Sometimes there were errors; the passengers in his moonship – a projectile launched from a huge cannon – would have been killed by acceleration forces, but the shell itself would have reached escape velocity.

The importance of Verne in rocket history lies in that his stories had a world-wide distribution, and numbers of scientists and inventors were set thinking by them. Of these, three men stand out as fathers of modern space-flight: a Russian, Konstantin Eduardovich Tsiolkowsky; an American, Robert H. Goddard, and a German, Hermann Oberth. Tsiolkowsky was a mathematician and a schoolteacher. His work was entirely theoretical, but extremely thorough. He knew that only a reaction engine would function in space, and accordingly worked out the thrust developed by a number of rocket propellants. His conclusion was that liquid oxygen, liquid hydrogen and kerosene, would be among the best to use. These have since been employed in the *Saturn* range of boosters.

Goddard's interest was not so much in Space Travel but in investigation of the upper atmosphere and Space by probe rocket. In contrast to the Russian theoretician, Goddard built and fired rockets to test his calculations. Like the Russian, he was painstaking. Although he knew that rockets work better in a vacuum, this theory was not enough, and he rigged up experiments to prove it. He continued in this way, step by step – first with powder rockets, later with liquid-fuel rockets.

In 1926, a strange, ten-foot-high device powered by petrol and liquid oxygen made the world's first liquid-fuel rocket ascent, rising 184 feet at a speed of 64 m.p.h. The motor was positioned at the top, connected to the fuel tanks below by slender tubes through which were conveyed the propellants. Goddard used this configuration because he thought that, by putting the weight of fuel below the 'push', this would make for stability. Only later did he realise that a rocket's flight is always in line with the direction of the exhaust. A number of rockets followed this first experiment and, by 1935, one had flown 1½ miles high at a speed of 700 m.p.h.

The odd thing about this period in rocket history is that none of the chief exponents knew much of what the others had done. As little was known of Tsiolkowsky's writing outside Russia, Hermann Oberth was acclaimed as the innovator of liquid-fuel rockets after the publication of his book, *'The Rocket into Interplanetary Space',* despite the fact that Goddard was already at that time testing his first motor.

One unexpected result of Oberth's book was that a famous German film director employed Oberth as technical director on a picture called *'The Girl in the Moon'*, which pleased the newly-formed Society for Space Travel for the publicity it provided.

Although each belatedly learnt of the other's work, there was little exchange of ideas.

The American scientist Robert Goddard, early investigator of the upper atmosphere

German scientist Hermann Oberth (below) was acclaimed as the inventor of the liquid fuel rocket. This was following publication of his book on interplanetary space in which he dealt with a number of advanced questions such as spacesuits and sleeping arrangements in a passenger carrying ship

Speed

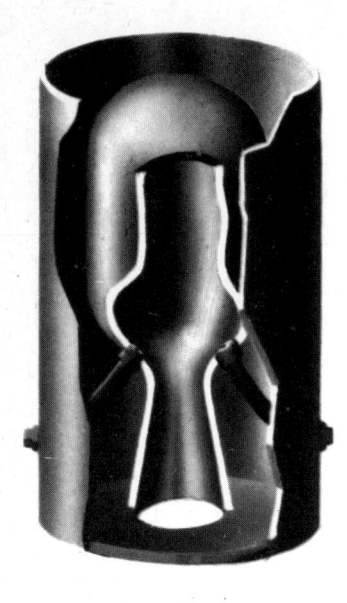

Theoretically, it would seem that to obtain fast speeds with rockets one has merely to use the propellant with the most energy, but in practice it is not so simple. Faster exhaust velocities mean higher temperatures in the combustion chamber, and there are limits imposed by the melting points of the material of which the chamber is made.

In the *V–2*, the alcohol and liquid oxygen used should ideally have produced an exhaust velocity nearly twice as fast as the actual speed, but if this had been allowed the firing chamber would have melted. Steel melts in the region of 1,300 degrees centigrade, and alcohol and lox (liquid oxygen) developing their maximum velocity would have generated a temperature nearer 9,000 degrees, so to keep the temperature within manageable limits the alcohol was adulterated to slow down its burning rate. Even reducing the exhaust velocity by half only decreased the combustion temperature to 3,000 degrees, but by using an efficient cooling system this could be contained.

Using all the cooling and protecting techniques to attain high speed is not enough for rockets which have to go into orbit around the earth or escape its attraction altogether, for yet another factor has to be taken into account – mass-ratio.

Mass-ratio is the ratio, or comparison, between the weight of the rocket fully fuelled, ready for take-off, and its weight when all the fuel has been burnt. For example, if a fuelled rocket weighs 100 tons on the launch pad, and 75 tons of that are fuel, its empty weight will be 25 tons. The full rocket weighs four times an empty one, so its mass-ratio is said to be four.

The mass-ratios of most single rockets are not much higher than this. If it were possible to build a rocket with a mass-ratio of about 40, the engineers' task would be simplified, but there is a snag. The weight of the empty rocket includes the weight of

*The **VfR Repulsor** motor was immersed in a water jacket in an attempt to keep it cool (fuel and liquid oxygen were sprayed through the pipes from below).*

Other methods of dealing with the high temperatures in the combustion chamber were lining the throat of the motor with heat resistant materials like tungsten or graphite or 'ablative coolings' – i.e. coating the metal with special plastics which melt, burn and vaporise in intense heat carrying away some of the heat as they do so. This is the same technique as used on the heat-resistant bases of manned capsules

Liquid and Solid Fuels

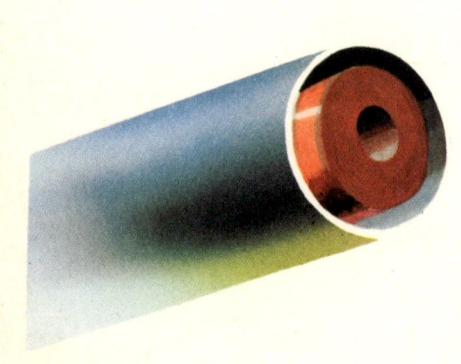

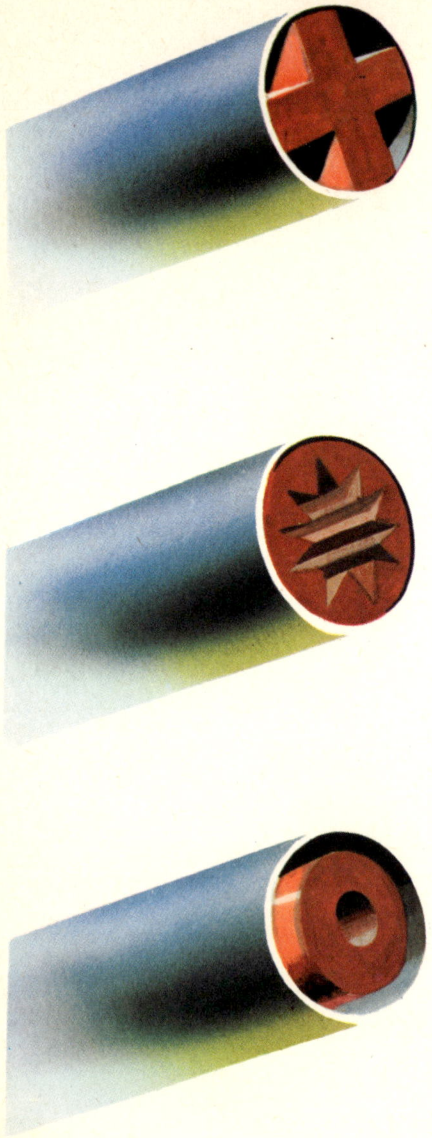

Solid fuel charges known as the 'Grain'. The simple hole through the charge could be many shapes. Here star and cross shaped channels give increased burning surface and assist rapid, even burning. Charges are cased in steel, titanium, fibre-glass or plastic-dipped glass thread – materials which can contain the pressure generated by combustion

The development of the liquid-fuel rocket was significant in rocket history, largely because the fuels that provide the most 'push' – those with the highest specific impulse – come in liquid form. Liquid-fuel combustion can be stopped by cutting off the supply of fuel, and restarted by reversing the process – an undoubted asset when flying complicated trajectories such as those that take a spacecraft into a 'parking orbit' before resuming its flight. Solid-fuel thrust can be stopped by 'blow off ports'; these are parts of the casing which are explosively blown off, thus allowing the gases to expand sideways instead of through the nozzle. However, this system removes any possibility of restarting the rocket.

Solid fuel has one military advantage – its instant readiness, as there is no long wait while the rocket is fuelled. Liquid propellants can be divided into storable and non-storable kinds. Storable ones, such as alcohol, hydrogen peroxide and nitric acid, can be kept in the rocket's tanks. *The Titan I* missile used one storable and one non-storable kind and it required about ten minutes to launch. The *Titan II*, using only storable fuels, needs one minute. Even so, solid fuels are easier to deal with.

Research continues in the search for more powerful solid fuels, which would presumably be used either for anti-missile missiles or in boosters such as those employed in the *Titan IIIc* configuration, which was intended to put a manned laboratory into orbit.

Although the liquid-fuel motor is more flexible, because not only can it be stopped and restarted but thrust can be varied as in a motor car by passing more or less fuel to the engine, more can go wrong with it. To get the fuel to the firing chamber, it must

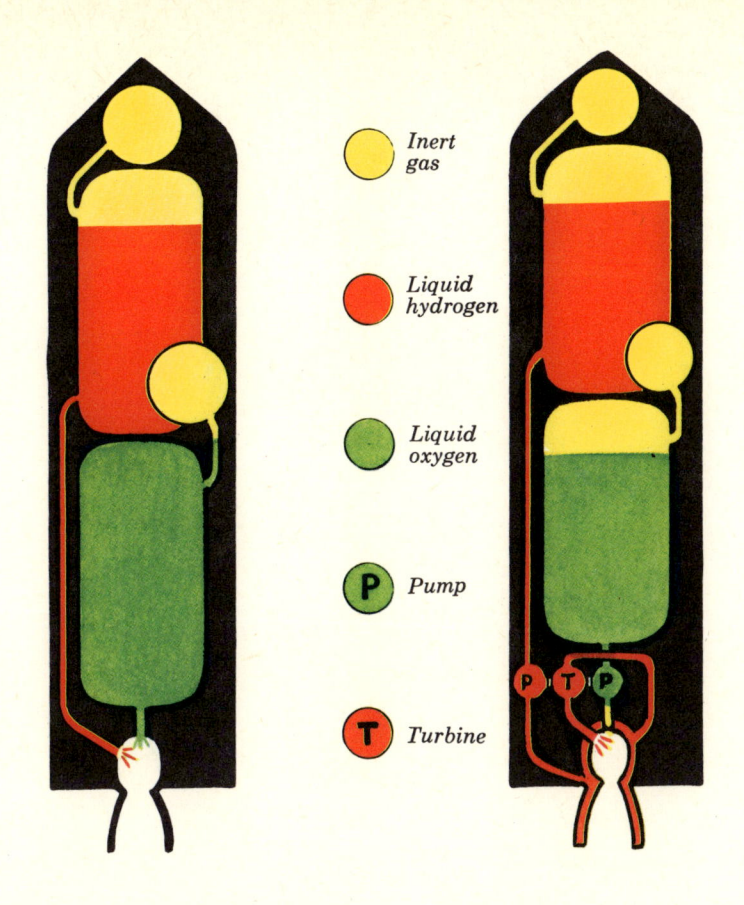

Left: A liquid oxygen, liquid hydrogen motor. The hydrogen and oxygen are pumped from the propellant tanks into the combustion chamber, where they burn. The liquid fuel first circulates through pipes surrounding the nozzle, providing the cooling necessary to prevent the nozzle melting
Below: **Titan IIIc,** *intended to put a manned laboratory into orbit*

either be pumped or forced in the right direction by pressure of an inert gas such as helium. The latter system is limited in practical application to low-thrust levels and short burning times; the majority of the big boosters such as *Saturn* use the pumping system. An examination of a liquid oxygen, liquid hydrogen motor, reveals how cunningly it is designed. The hydrogen – liquid at −423 degrees Faherenheit and contained under pressure – is allowed to force its way through the fuel inlet valve and the fuel pump and then moves through pipes surrounding the exhaust nozzle (which would otherwise melt), the heat passing to the hydrogen raising its temperature to −100 degrees. Now in gaseous form, the hydrogen expands through a turbine which drives pumps on both propellant fuel lines. Further refinements allow the turbine to be bypassed should the thrust increase too much, thus reducing propellant flow rate. It says much for the engineering of modern boosters that most of them work perfectly – even the big ones that gulp tons of fuel per second.

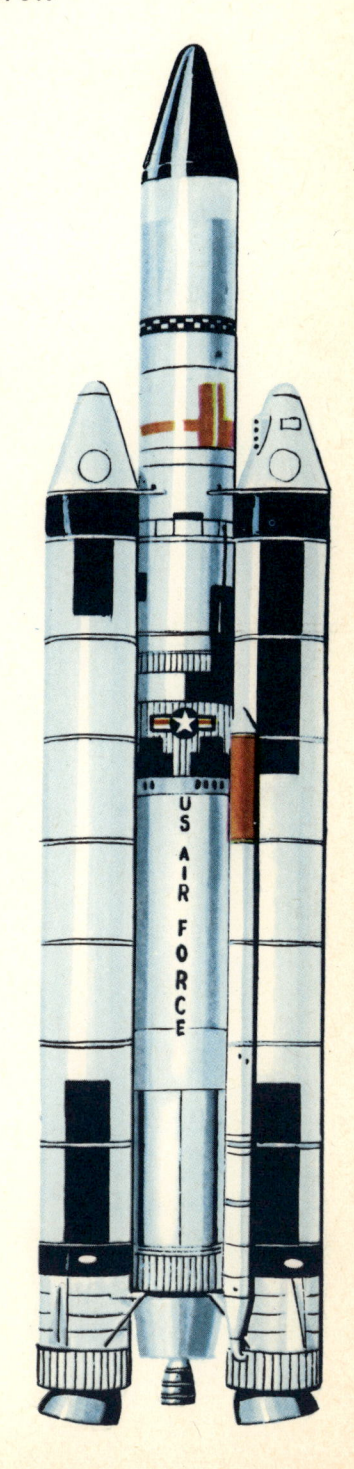

Guidance

A missile fired at a moving target, and a space vehicle entering a precise orbit after a near vertical take-off, both need guidance to make them turn to reach their objective. The inertial guidance system, geared to a computer with a programmed flight path, is a form of pre-set guidance.

In the case of a missile seeking a moving target such as an enemy tank, aeroplane or missile, the method used is usually command guidance. At its simplest, in, say, an anti-tank missile, fine wires are attached to it which unreel as it flies. Through these electrical impulses can be sent to activate the steering mechanisms, but the missile's range is limited to a mile or so. Above that distance it is more usual to use straightforward radio control.

Space vehicles are generally tracked throughout their flight, and course corrections radioed to the control mechanisms as needed. Radar is used in several ways to guide missiles from the ground, or the radar can be mounted in the missile, which then homes on the signals reflected from the target. But for this the missile has to carry equipment which leaves less of the total payload available for the warhead.

Command guidance being used to send a missile to hit a moving target. Fine wires attached to the missile unreel it as it flies enabling electric impulses to be sent through them to steer the missile towards its target. Radar from the ground tracks the moving target and the missile. A radio receiver in the missile keeps the projectile centred in a radio beam that is focussed on the target in the system known as 'beam rider guidance'

Another homing device is the heat sensor, which can detect infra-red waves from jet engines and missile exhausts. The message is passed electrically to the steering mechanism, so that the missile follows the target. Another system deals with a missile intended for a target, say in an enemy country. As the missile flies overland, it takes a continuous radar picture of the terrain, matching what it sees with an accurate coded tape of what it should see when on course. Should the two 'pictures' not match, the missile alters course until the match is exact.

The attitude, or the way a spacecraft is pointing, can be very important when it is desired to alter course by a thrust in a new direction, or when the capsule must 'hit' the atmosphere at the right angle so that part of it designed to bear the intense heat of atmospheric friction does so. Small subsidiary nozzles positioned on the rocket or capsule are used to rotate it around its centre of gravity. The *Atlas* missile has two such small motors, called verniers, mounted just above its ribbed booster 'skirt'. These can swivel in any direction to alter the angle of attack. The attitude jets on the *Mercury* and subsequent capsules owe much to experience gained from using those fitted to the nose and wingtips of the *X–15*, a manned research rocket plane.

*Stellar guidance being used to orientate space-probe **Mariner 4** in space. Because they are so far away stars appear to stay in the same place relative to a craft moving in the solar system. This is made use of by aligning telescopes on to suitable stars, (Space-probe **Mariner 4** used the Sun and **Canopus**, a star) so that the rocket's attitude may be controlled to keep it in the correct position*

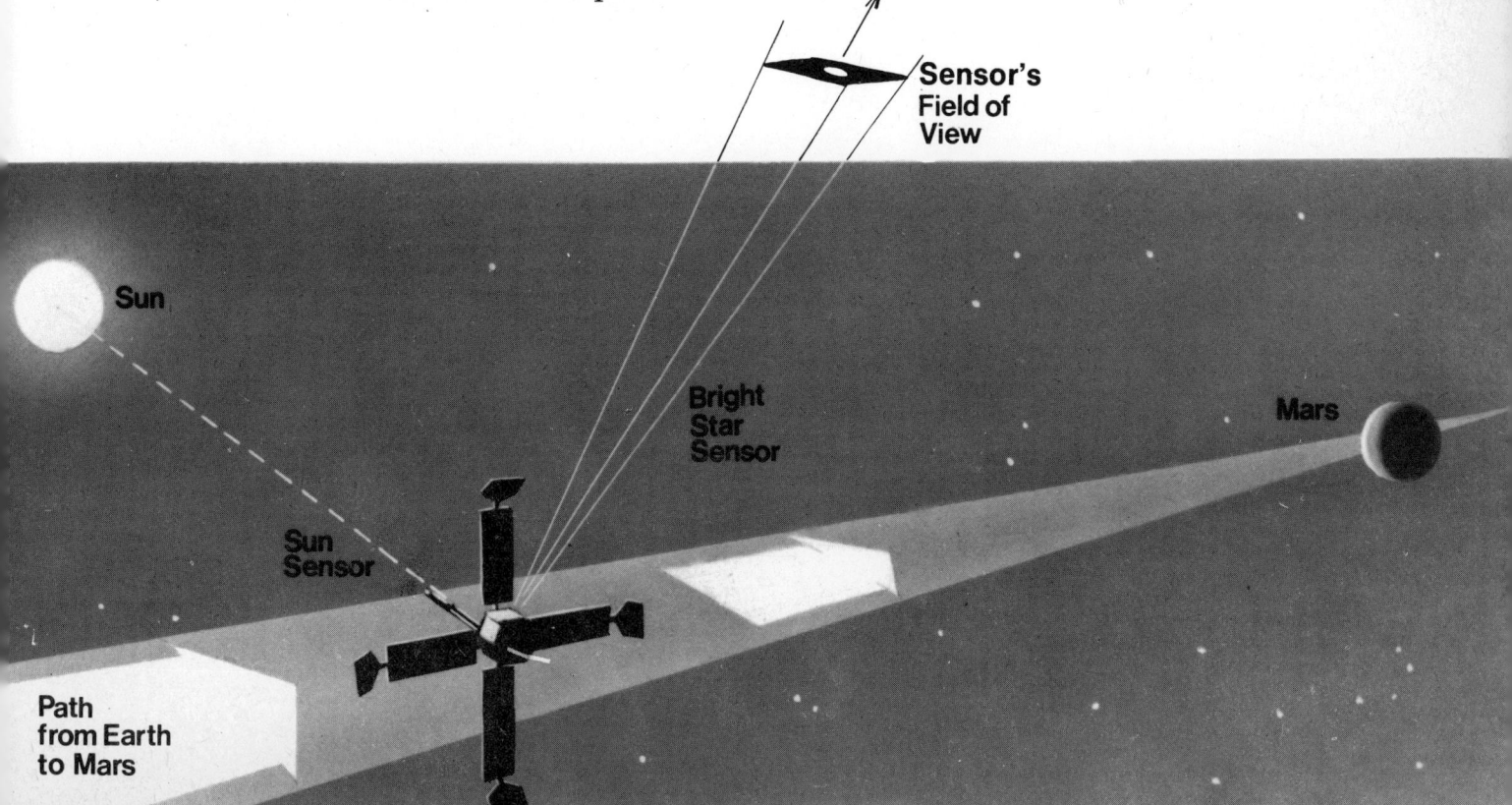

Performance

Nozzle shapes in order of effectiveness. Simple hole, divergent, convergent, convergent divergent, expansion cone

No matter how well a rocket performs, designers always seek ways to improve it. Broadly speaking, their job consists of achieving a nice balance between the power of the motor and the weight it must move at the correct speed to do its job.

A rocket's speed depends on the amount of gas ejected and the speed at which the gas leaves the nozzle – called exhaust velocity. The amount of gas leaving the rocket each second is called thrust, and it is this figure which indicates how much weight the motor will lift. This is very important in a launch vehicle which has to overcome the force of gravity, as can be seen if one imagines a hypothetical rocket, built by the proverbial mad professor, weighing ten tons and with a thrust of ten tons. On being ignited such a rocket would support its own weight but it would not leave the launch pad. Now a large part of any rocket's weight is that of the fuel, and, as this is consumed, the weight of the rocket is reduced. Although thrust can be varied, it is usually constant, so after a time our rocket would begin to move as the ten-ton thrust lifted the rocket which now weighed less than ten tons. Here the law of inertia complicates the picture, for just as moving objects such as the gyroscope wheel tend to stay in the same position, so a body at rest tends to remain in the same place. This would have to be overcome by more work from the motor, and the upshot is that the mad professor's brainchild would rise only a few feet in the air before falling back to the ground. In practice there is usually a generous margin left between launch weight and thrust, as can be seen from the following figures for the *Apollo Saturn,* which has a launch weight in round figures of 2,678 tons and a launch thrust of 3,348 tons.

The speed at which the gas leaves the rocket – its exhaust velocity – governs the speed of the rocket. Newton's *Third Law of Motion* puts this in a nutshell in stating that 'For every action, there is an equal and opposite reaction.' The exhaust velocity depends on the effectiveness of the fuel used, or its specific impulse. This is measured by finding the amount of thrust produced when a pound of the propellant is burned in one second. But the design of the nozzle can affect the speed of ejection. As the fuel burns it forms a gas which expands at a fixed rate. Given the same rate of expansion, a smaller hole – or venturi, as it is called – results in a faster exhaust velocity.

Now a gas expanding through a hole into a region of lower pressure will naturally tend to expand in all directions once through the hole. The nozzle, therefore, has a cone-shaped extension added (known as an expansion cone) which reduces the wasteful sideways expansion by directing it backwards.

Rockets in order of ascending size drawn to scale with an average house. From left: **V2(A-4), Atlas Centaur, Gemini Titan, Saturn I and Saturn V** *(for weights and thrust figures see layout)*

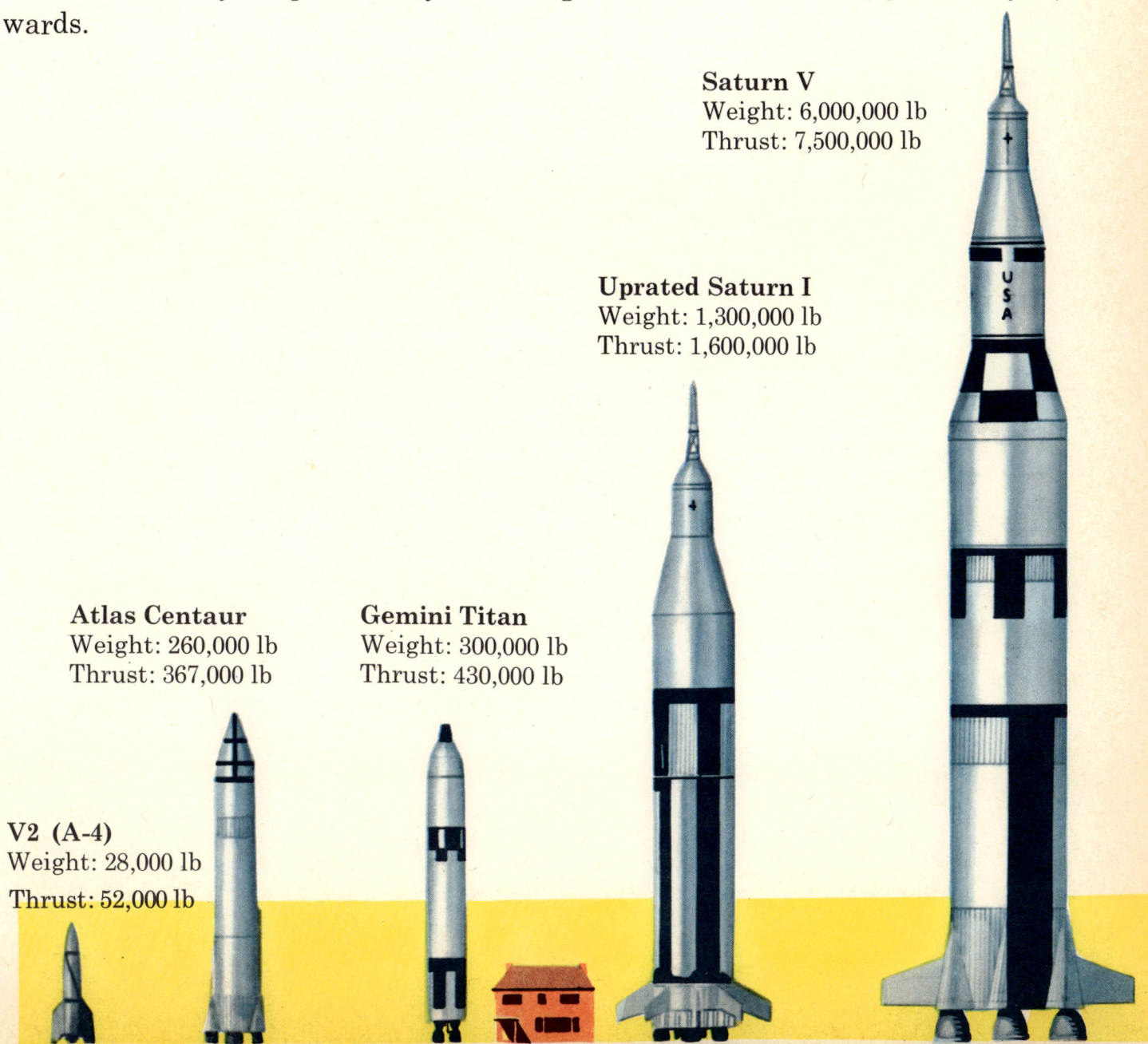

Saturn V
Weight: 6,000,000 lb
Thrust: 7,500,000 lb

Uprated Saturn I
Weight: 1,300,000 lb
Thrust: 1,600,000 lb

Atlas Centaur
Weight: 260,000 lb
Thrust: 367,000 lb

Gemini Titan
Weight: 300,000 lb
Thrust: 430,000 lb

V2 (A-4)
Weight: 28,000 lb
Thrust: 52,000 lb

the structure of the rocket and the tanks that hold the fuel, so that as fast as one increases the amount of fuel, which would improve the mass-ratio, one also has to add the weight of the fuel tanks and structure to contain that fuel, which lowers the mass-ratio.

On the other hand, as the fuel is used up there is an increasing weight of useless metal in the fuel tanks. What is wanted is a rocket that improves its mass-ratio as it flies by shedding the weight of empty fuel tankage and the structure which connects it to the rest of the rocket. This sounds impossible, but the result is achieved by using a multi-stage rocket, which, in effect, throws away useless weight stage by stage as these burn out.

Regarding each stage separately, these can each be built with a mass-ratio of 5, the bottom stage reaching 8,000 m.p.h. The payload of this stage is another smaller rocket, again with the same mass-ratio, which will add another 8,000 m.p.h., making 16,000; the third stage is the payload of the second, adding another 8,000 m.p.h. Total, 24,000 m.p.h. – sufficient to put the final stage into orbit round the Earth even after allowing for air drag and other losses.

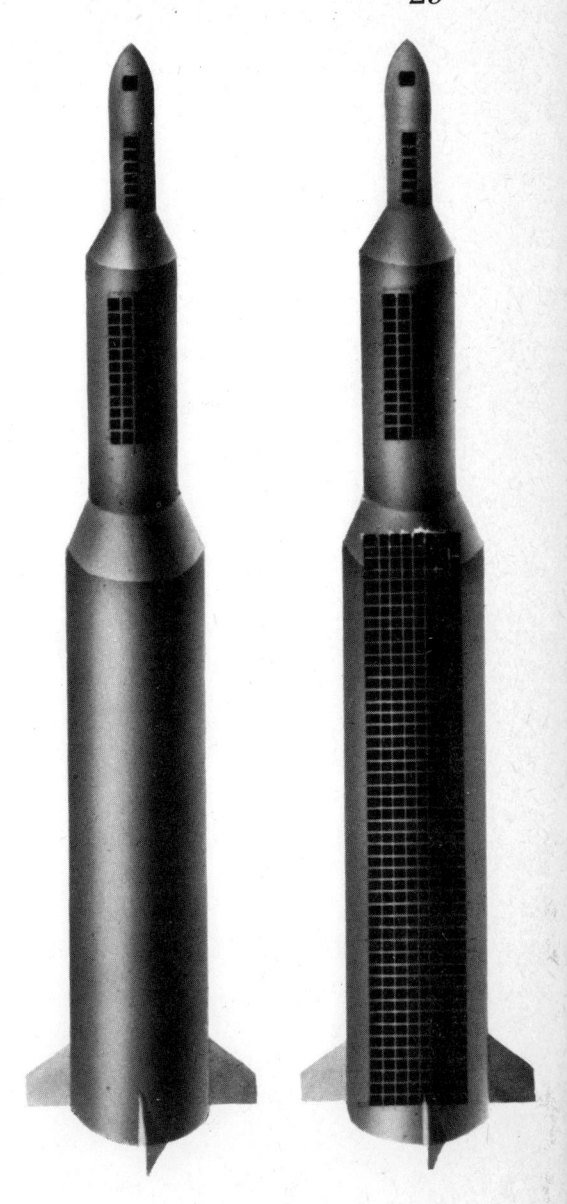

Building a three stage rocket with a mass ratio of five. The first stage can reach 8,000 m.p.h., the second stage 16,000 m.p.h. and the third stage can reach 24,000 m.p.h.

Steering and Stability

Making sure that a rocket flies in the right direction throughout its flight is a problem that has exercised the minds of rocket men from the Chinese onwards. Spin stabilization works satisfactorily for small missiles. These usually have tailfins set at a slight angle to impart spinning motion. Some missiles are even simpler in that their tailfins are set straight, like arrow feathers. However, while fins keep a rocket straight, they cannot correct a deviation caused by a gust of wind and, if the rocket is tilted from its correct path, the fins may keep it straight on the new, wrong heading. Also, fins only work where there is sufficient air to act on aerodynamic surfaces.

The light rockets of the early experimenters were all too easily deflected, as Goddard found. His solution was to deflect the exhaust to one side or the other by graphite vanes tough enough to withstand the heat and blast. To move the vanes as required, Goddard made use of a gyroscope.

Inertial guidance is a more sophisticated development of Goddard's system. A person in a car which brakes suddenly would, unless restrained by a belt, be thrown forward, because his inertia tends to keep him moving at the speed of the car before it braked. Inertial guidance uses this tendency in three devices called accelerometers, which measure the motion of the rocket in three directions – up-and-down, forwards-and-backwards, and sideways and can redirect it.

Goddard's method of steering. In Goddard's rocket the gyroscope's resistance to being tilted was harnessed to valves. These when opened allowed gas under pressure into cylinders where it pushed pistons. These were connected to the vanes which deflected the exhaust and brought the rocket back on course. A more sophisticated development of this same principle is used on spaceships today

Gyroscopes form the basis of most sophisticated guidance systems. Once set spinning they tend to remain pointing in the same direction no matter how much their mounting is deflected

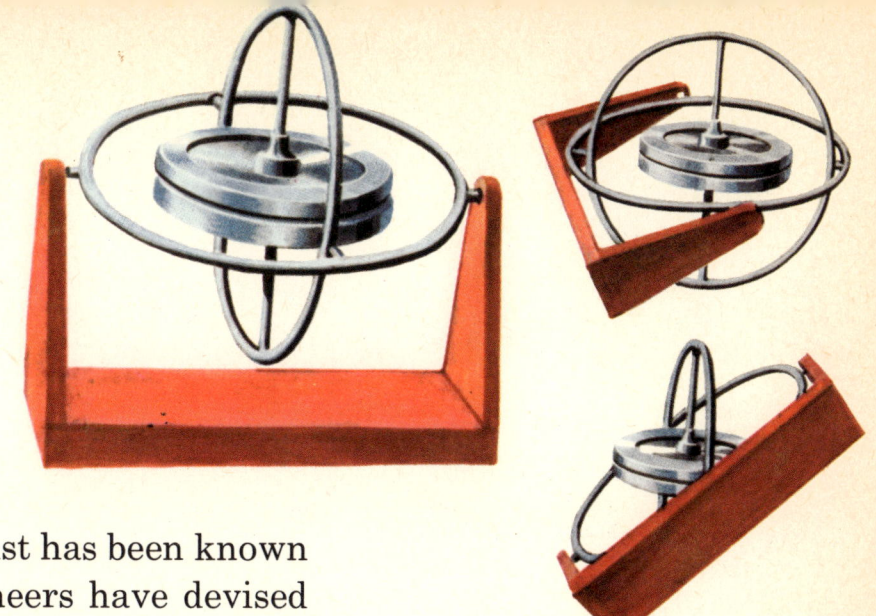

The heat and blast of the exhaust has been known to break even graphite, so engineers have devised differing methods of steering. One way is to mount the whole engine on gimbals, so that it can turn a few degrees in any direction. Then there is the jetavator – a circular ring mounted inside the nozzle which acts in the same manner as the vanes. Another ring device is a hollow tube in which there are a number of holes. Through these a fluid (gas or liquid) is squirted from a few holes at a time. When the fluid meets the jet stream, a shockwave is set up which deflects the exhaust in the desired direction according to which holes the fluid was initially squirted from.

These devices, all of which work as well in space as in the atmosphere, correct the course automatically. But, as we shall see, the commands that control the rocket's steering mechanism need not derive from the rocket's own motion.

An inertial guidance platform in which the accelerometers are mounted on a platform held stable by gyroscopes acting in three directions to the platform. The measurements made by the accelerometers are relayed to a computer which eventually re-directs the rocket

Different principles of deflection. 1, By a circular ring mounted inside the nozzle 2, By a fluid (gas or liquid) injection and 3, By mounting the engine on gimbals to enable it to turn in any direction

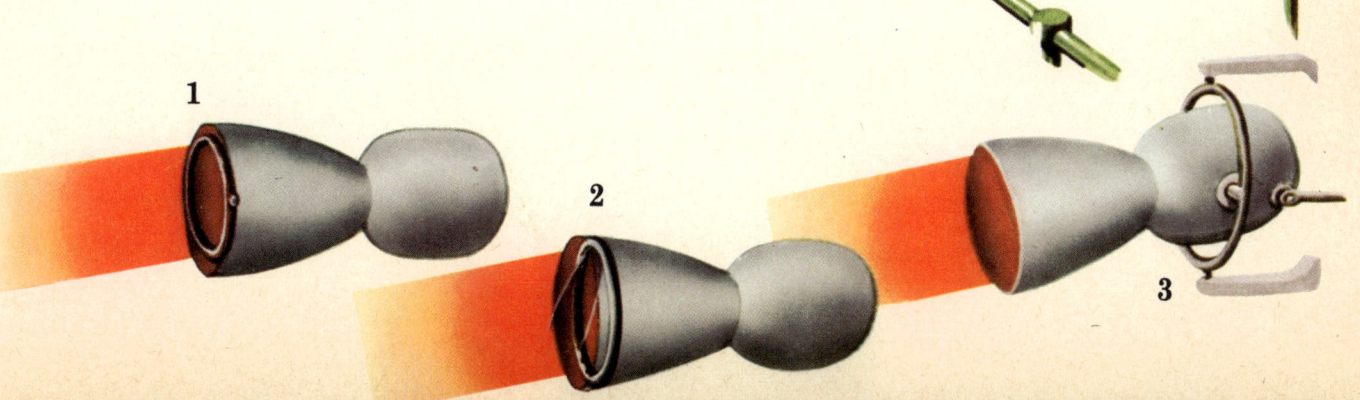

Sounding Rockets

*Above, the **Montgolfier** balloon, designed in 1783, carried thermometers, barometers, hygrometers and bottles to be filled with high altitude air for analysis*

Military necessity, rather than scientific enquiry, led to the development of the *V–2* rocket missile. On September 8th, 1944, the first *V–2* bomb dropped on London and opened up a new phase in weaponry that is still being developed. By the standards of its time this was a giant of a rocket, 46 feet in height, weighing twelve tons and carrying a one-ton warhead. The *V–2* and its creator, von Braun, had started mankind on its road to the stars.

American scientists moved in as soon as the German rocket installations were captured and those German scientists and technicians who would co-operate, and all the remaining stocks of rockets, were moved to America. There Wernher von Braun was put in charge of development at Redstone Arsenal.

The first of the modified *V–2* missiles that had been instrumented for research into the upper atmosphere took off from the U.S. Army's base at White Sands in June, 1946. It carried a geiger-counter telescope to detect and record cosmic ray activity, pressure gauges, temperature gauges and special radio transmitters to probe the ionosphere. Over the next six years, 60 more *V–2's* were fired directly upwards over ranges between 50 and 100 miles.

By this time the supply of *V–2* parts had dried up and new research had led to the development of the all-American sounding rocket vehicle, known as the *Wac Corporal*. It was smaller than the *V–2*, ran on nitric acid and aniline liquid propellants and had a simplified control and guidance system.

It was, in fact, a prototype of the many kinds of sounding rocket used nowadays for meteorological research projects. These are simple, instrument-

*The **Viking,** America's first fully steerable ground controlled big rocket, on the launching pad being checked over before it made its 135 mile second flight. The payload of instruments and radio-controlled, gyroscopically actuated steering gear weighed a lot less than the ton of war-head the V–2 had been designed to carry so the performance was higher*

packed probes which, when launched with suitable solid-fuelled boosters, can operate at heights of up to 2,000 miles and send back their findings by radio. Under ground control they can release chemicals, return instrument packages by parachute, check radiation conditions, measure wind speeds and televise hurricanes from above.

In fact, the new information gathered by these probes has told us more about the earth we live on than the space around it. The sampling, testing and reaction probing of such rocket vehicles has given us valuable information and warnings about the man-made changes in our atmospheric environment brought about by pollution on a grand scale. The V–2 weapon has thus developed into a tool for the benefit of all mankind.

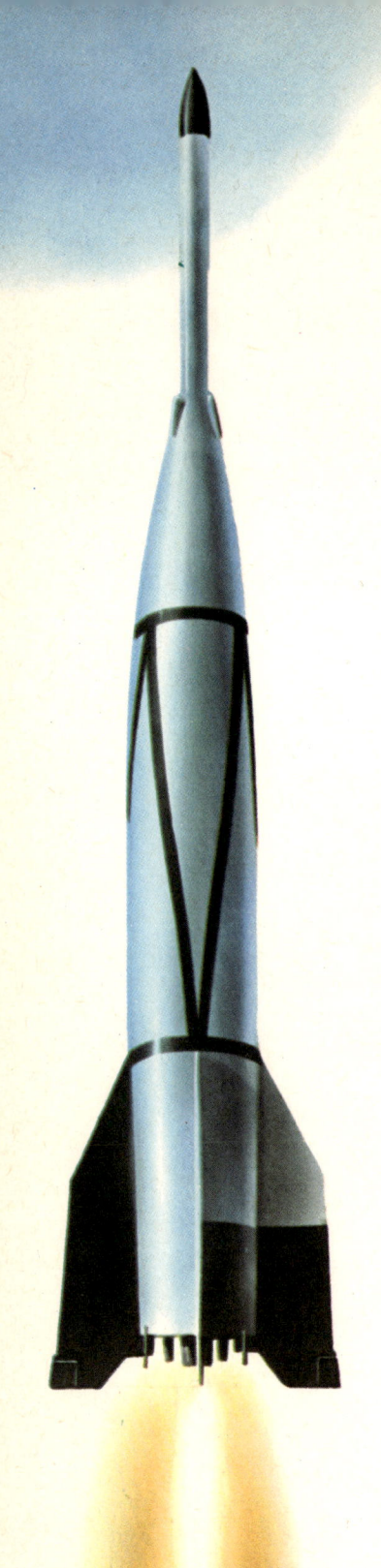

The Beginning of the Big Ones

If the *V–2* and *Wac Corporal* missiles showed the practical possibilities of rocket propulsion for space exploration, they also showed the short-comings of the vehicles themselves. The liquid-fuelled power units put the rockets aloft, but once the fuel ran out they were left to their own devices. They kept on going upwards and onwards, but they rolled and tumbled about in a way that made camera observation virtually useless.

So the next phase was the design of a fully-steerable, ground-controlled vehicle, and the first of these was the *Viking*. It was smaller and slimmer than the *V–2*, being only 37 feet long by 30 inches diameter and weighing under 5 tons fully loaded.

Although rocket and missile development in the United States was, and still is, under the control of the armed forces, the *Viking* was designed for upper atmosphere exploration rather than missile carrying. By getting a package of the right instruments 150 miles or so above the earth, the causes and characteristics of weather variations could be studied more effectively in a few minutes than was possible in years of observation at ground level. Accurate forecasting improved naval efficiency, and the Navy had more use for weather probes than for missiles in 1946.

Probably more people talk about the weather than any other single subject, but very few know anything about it. Radio operators have been concerned about the unpredictable behaviour of their communications and blame the ionosphere. Astronomers hate the ozone screen some 20 miles or so above the earth's surface that cuts off so much of the light reaching the earth. In attempts to study the atmosphere better, our observatories have been built on high mountains or towers, but the first big jump upwards came with balloons.

The Montgolfier balloon, designed in 1783, carried thermometers, barometers, hygrometers and bottles to be filled with high-altitude air for analysis. More varied instruments were carried in other balloon flights during the nineteenth century. In 1875, however, two scientists lost their lives while climbing from Paris to a height of 28,000 feet without oxygen. After that, unmanned balloons (*Ballons Sondes*) began to be used.

The first *Viking* climbed 50 miles in May, 1949; *Viking 4* reached 105 miles; *Viking 11* set up a record of 158 miles; and, more important to the prestige of American rocketry, all design objectives had been achieved.

The *Vikings* were built for the *Naval Research Laboratory* by Glenn Martin, with a 21,000-lb.-thrust rocket motor built by Reaction Motors, Inc. Development work had proceeded from the design stage with hardly a hitch. In fact, only one static test failure marred the programme. Not surprisingly, the Americans felt confident about their space programme and planned to celebrate the International Geophysical Year in 1957 by launching an instrumented satellite. A successor to *Viking*, called *Vanguard,* was planned, built and flown in October, 1957. But they were too late. The Russians had got there first. *Sputnik I* was already in orbit.

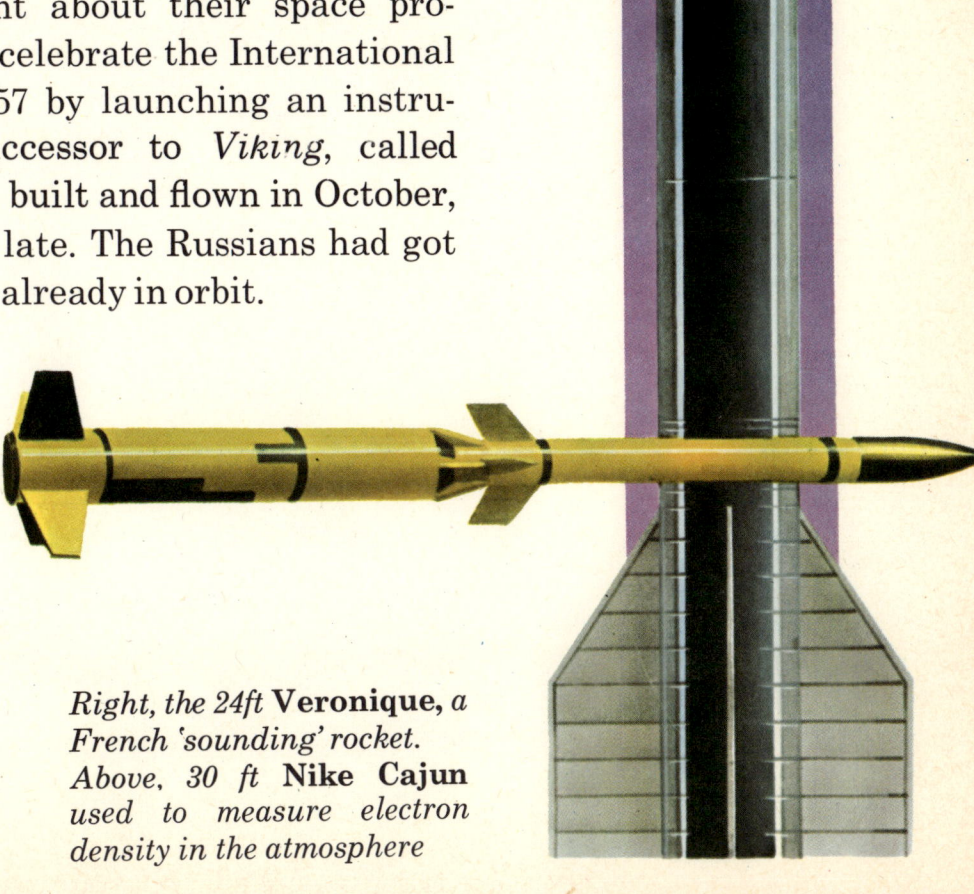

Left, **Aerobee**, *an instrument-packed probe used for meteorological research.*

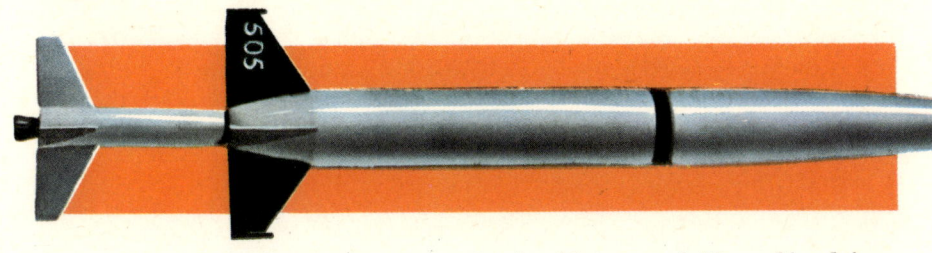

Right, the 24ft **Veronique***, a French 'sounding' rocket. Above, 30 ft* **Nike Cajun** *used to measure electron density in the atmosphere*

Work Horses

Not all rockets get the acclaim they deserve; some serve well in the fields of research and development but never get their names in print. Most people recognise the names *Viking, Vanguard* and *Saturn* as rockets that have played their part in the American side of the space race, but few have ever heard of *Redstone, Scout* or *Little Joe*.

Scout, for example, is a rocket that proved what did not work. In the purely military field, all development on ground-to-ground and ground-to-air missiles was firmly based on solid-fuel propellants. The rocket could be fully fuelled up and then stored, ready for firing in a 'hard' launching site if required. The propellent remained stable to the extent that a fully-fuelled rocket could be moved around. Most importantly, the size and weight of the launching vehicle, thrust for thrust, was higher than for a liquid-fuelled type.

These are all very definite advantages in practical military terms, and it is not surprising that the U.S. Army tried out the possibilities of solid fuel when it came to building the big rockets for entry into space. The liquid-fuelled rocket has to be filled afresh for each launch and the filling itself is a tense procedure with considerable risks involved. It takes time and quite a lot of manpower to fuel up. The bodies of the rockets have to be strong, which usually means heavy. All these factors underline the superiority of the solid-fuelled rockets, but there is another side to the story. It is very difficult to get a really large solid-fuel chamber to burn through

Little Joe... *was used whenever short flight tests were required. For example it was used during the* **Apollo** *escape system test in 1965*

Scout... *a four stage all-solid-fuelled rocket capable of putting a 240 lb satellite into orbit over 300 miles up. The first stage was gyro guided and the fourth spin stabilized to hold it on course*

Redstone ... *was originally developed from the wartime* **V2** *by the Wernher von Braun team and used from 1956 as a launching rocket. It launched Commander Shepard in the* **Mercury** *spacecraft* **Freedom 7** *on the first American manned sub-orbital flight*

evenly, and control of fuel flow and power output is limited.

Nevertheless, the lessons learned from *Scout*, a four-stage all solid-fuelled rocket, gave the big solid-fuelled rocket a place in the sun later in the space race. The two solid-fuelled boosters that are strapped on each side of the liquid-fuelled *Titan III* are developments of the *Scout*.

Redstone was another rocket that did an enormous amount of background work but rarely got itself into the news. It has been superseded by the *Pershing* for military use. In the space field the *Redstone* was developed into the *Jupiter–C,* which showed its capabilities by sending a substantial payload over 3,400 miles across the Atlantic in September, 1956.

In the *Mercury* programme, a *Redstone* rocket carried Commander Shepard to a height of 155 miles and reached a peak speed of 5,100 m.p.h.

Perhaps the least known of all the rockets which have participated in the American space programme is *Little Joe*. This small, stubby-looking rocket has been used for years whenever short-flight tests of space vehicles or components have been required.

Astronauts at the top of *Saturn's* 360-foot column can rest secure that in the event of an explosion or malfunction on take-off, the escape rocket that will carry them clear owes its development to work done by the 40-foot *Little Joe*.

Atlas

The *Intercontinental Ballistic Missile* is a device for throwing a warhead accurately at a target which may be many thousands of miles away. Power is essential to such a weapon's system, but control is equally essential. A bearing only half a degree off course at launching would put the missile many miles off target at the end of 6,000 miles or so, and guidance systems have to be very fast and very accurate to deal with an object that is streaking away from its base at 16,000 miles an hour.

These were the problems facing the American engineers when they set out to design the *Atlas* missile.

The *Atlas* rocket system was and is unusual in that the main engine is supported by two smaller booster engines which are jettisoned two minutes after take-off, but all fire together for the launch. In addition there are two small vernier motors designed for precise speed control. These continue to operate under ground control after the missile's main rocket has cut off. Then the verniers shut off with the missile dead on target; the nose-cone (warhead) blows off by retro-rockets and finishes the flight in unguided ballistic trajectory.

Atlas is still in demand as a satellite launcher. The smooth, controlled take-off has made it particularly suitable as a launching rocket for manned flights. Colonel Glenn and Commander Schirra were both *Atlas*-borne when they made their orbital flights.

Atlas was also used as a first stage in the *Atlas-Agena* rocket assembly for the successful launching of the spacecraft *Mariner 2* on its voyage to *Venus* in 1962; four years later it played the same role in the *Atlas-Centaur* vehicle for the soft-landed moon shot, *Surveyor I*. Throughout its active life, the *Atlas* design has proved itself a reliable workhorse with a surprising degree of flexibility.

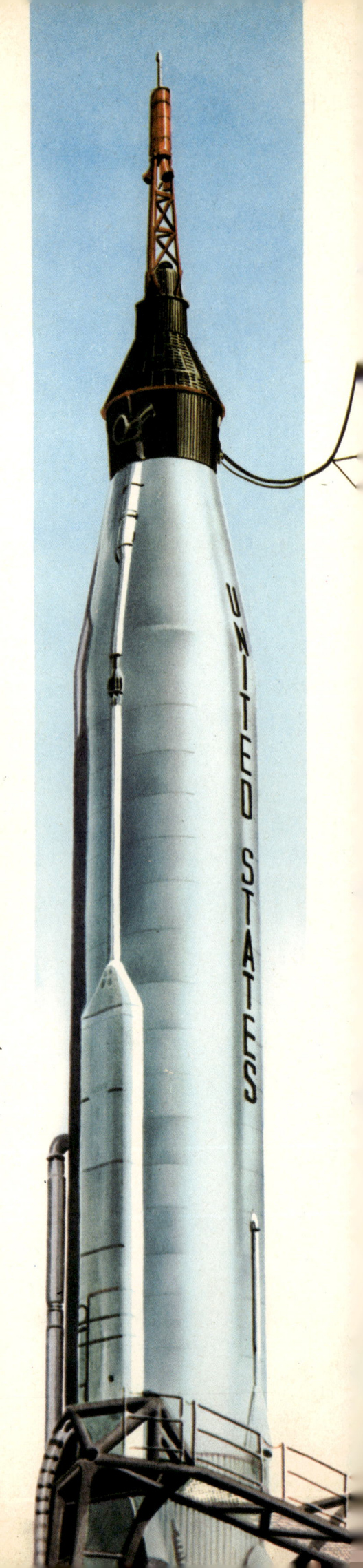

The U.S.A.F. *Able* launchings, which started with the *Thor* rocket as first-stage booster, switched to using *Atlas* in a four-stage assembly used for interplanetary probes from Cape Canaveral. The second stage is an *Aerojet* liquid-fuel engine: the third stage a solid-fuel engine as used in the *Vanguard*, and the fourth stage a special vehicle which brings the total length of the rocketry to 8 inches short of 100 feet.

Atlas also plays its part in the *Midas* anti-ICBM vehicles and the *Samos* reconnaissance satellite programme.

The *Atlas-Vega* rocket was developed by *Convair* for the National Aeronautics and Space Administration to provide a thoroughly reliable general-purpose vehicle with a variety of uses. It is a three-stage assembly, with a General Electric second stage and a *Vanguard* third, bringing the total length to 112 feet.

Its range of jobs covers putting a half-ton weather satellite into orbit over 300 miles up, a fixed orbit communications satellite weighing 740 lb. which travels at earth rotation speed and thus maintains one position relative to the surface, and a two-man space laboratory for a range of flight research projects. *Atlas* represents an important stage in the growing up of space technology – the design of a rocket that is no longer an experiment, but a readily available and reliable tool for the space travel industry to use.

The **Atlas** *is 75 feet long and 10 feet in diameter. Right is an artist's impression of the first successful test firing from* **Cape Canaveral** *in November 1958. The missile covered 6,325 miles.* **Atlas** *has today been replaced by more powerful rockets in the military field but it is still in demand as a satelite launcher*

Rocket Planes

Rockets and aeroplanes took a surprisingly long time to join forces. Rockets use up their fuel supplies very quickly compared with internal combustion engines, whether piston, turbine or jet. Aeroplanes, on the other hand, have always been visualised as vehicles for relatively long-distance travel. It was in the field of weaponry that the two concepts were first brought together.

The idea had been put forward as far back as 1908 by a French aviator named René Lorin, and 20 years later the Germans were trying out rocket-assisted gliders. In 1929 another German, von Opel, achieved 100 miles an hour in a ten minute flight with a rocket-powered plane. It was not until the end of 1944, however, that a rocket-propelled fighter plane appeared in the air – a German Messerschmitt Komet. Although it was by far the fastest climbing plane ever seen at that time, the Komet's flying time was only four minutes, and so its range and effectiveness were somewhat limited.

However, the practicability of a rocket plane had been demonstrated and when, in that same year, the U.S.A.F. decided to commission a design for supersonic flight, the choice of a power plant fell on rockets.

The *Bell X–1* first flew in 1946, with an engine that was totally enclosed in the after part of the fuselage. The plane weighed less than two-hundredweight, consisted of four rockets and offered a developed thrust of 6000 lb.

The launching system was designed to conserve the rocket power until the *Bell X–1* had reached a reasonable height for the supersonic speed attempt.

The German World War II **Viper** *rocket interceptor which was ramp launched The pilot was killed in the sole flight attempted*

The **Bell X-1A** *experimental plane. The series was concerned with high speeds and high altitudes. It was attached to the underside of a B 29 bomber and was taken up to 27,000 ft where it cut loose using its own power*

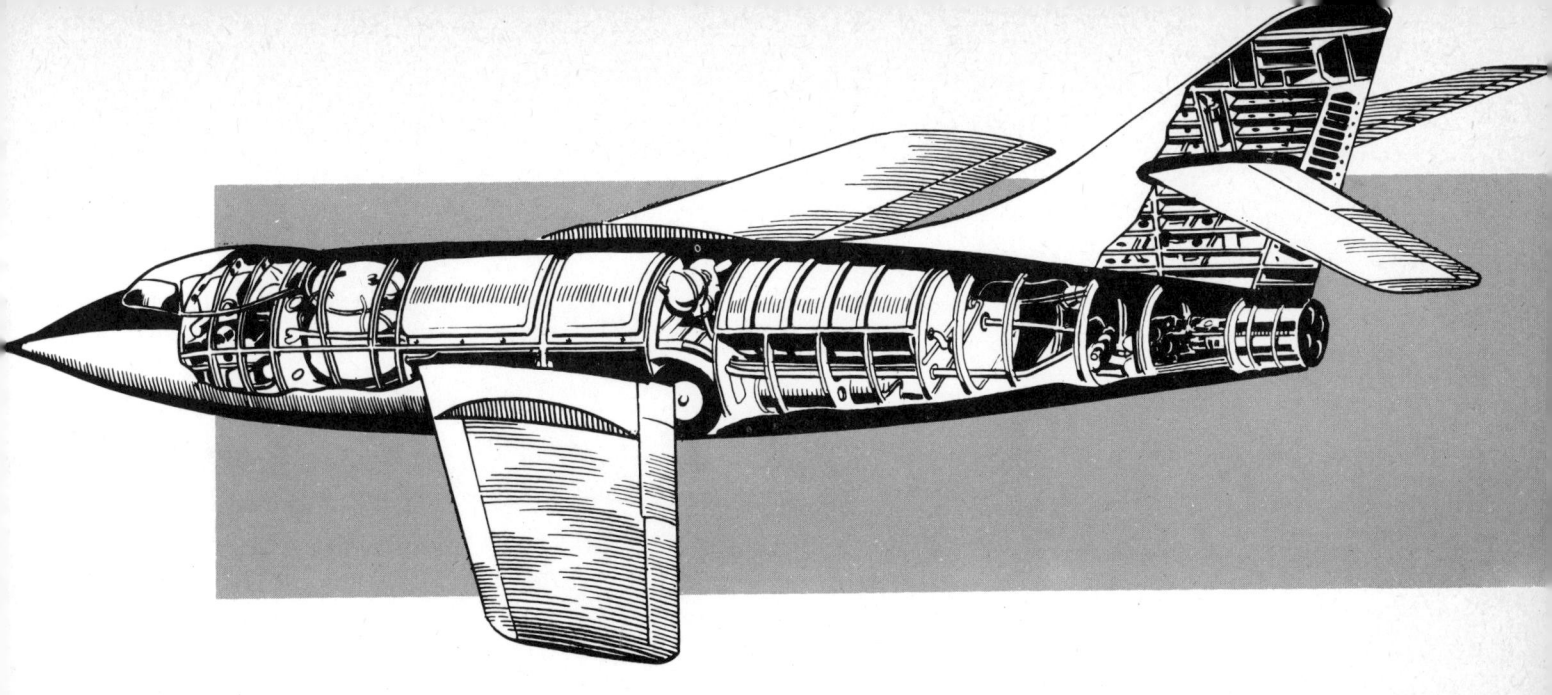

*The supersonic **Skyrocket** built by the U.S. Navy. It had a completely new power unit concept using both a turbo-jet and a rocket motor. In 1951 it achieved the record speed of 1,238 m.p.h. at an altitude of 79,000 feet*

First tests showed that the plane handled well, but it was not until its thirteenth flight – on October 14th, 1947 – that the speed target was achieved. The *X–1* flew faster than sound at 760 m.p.h.

Competition immediately hotted up, and the following year the Navy took a hand with their own supersonic plane, called Skyrocket. It had two motors, a turbo-jet which was capable of take-off, climb and high sub-sonic speeds on its 3,000-lb. thrust, and a 6,000-lb. thrust rocket motor. These boosted it on August 15th, 1951 to a new record speed of 1,238 m.p.h., at an altitude of no less than 79,000 feet.

Bell responded two years later – in December, 1953 – with a new version of the *X–1* called the *X–1A*, then beat their own record again in 1954 when an improved version, the *X–2*, set new standards for both speed and altitude with a shattering performance at Muroc Dry Lake of 2,200 m.p.h. and 126,000 feet.

Although all these aeroplanes were developed by and for the United States Air Force and Navy with purely military objectives in view, they were actually more in the nature of pure research projects, as they were unarmed and no definite strategic or tactical roles were envisaged for them.

What the *Bell X–1* and *X–2* and the Skyrocket plane did was to prove the efficiency of the rocket engine in the specialised sphere of ultra-high-speed and extreme high-altitude operation. This they did conclusively.

Rocket Planes

Early rocket planes were adapted aeroplanes. The next stage was to design specially for the rocket engine. The first of these craft to fly was the *Bell X–15*, which was more a piloted rocket than a rocket plane.

No practical use has yet been thought up for such ultra-high-speed mini-planes as the X–plane family. They are purely experimental designs that were built to find out the limits and possibilities of men and materials in stratosphere flight at several thousand miles an hour. Quite obviously, the cost/efficiency ratios of such craft as carriers prohibit their commercial application. The fuel used – anhydrous ammonia and liquid oxygen – is extremely expensive; a whole tankful lasts only a few minutes in flight, and the payload is virtually one man and his baggage.

But although the X–planes themselves have neither commercial value as carriers nor military value as weapons, and the project in this form has temporarily been shelved, the data obtained by the development and testing of the rocket planes has been useful in many ways.

The **X-15** *(below) has made many hundreds of flights and reached speeds in excess of six times the speed of sound. It is 50 feet long and has a wing span of only 22 feet. Almost half the length is taken up with the liquid fuel tanks which can be jettisoned when empty. The delta winged shape below is a designer's idea for a new version – still on the drawing board*

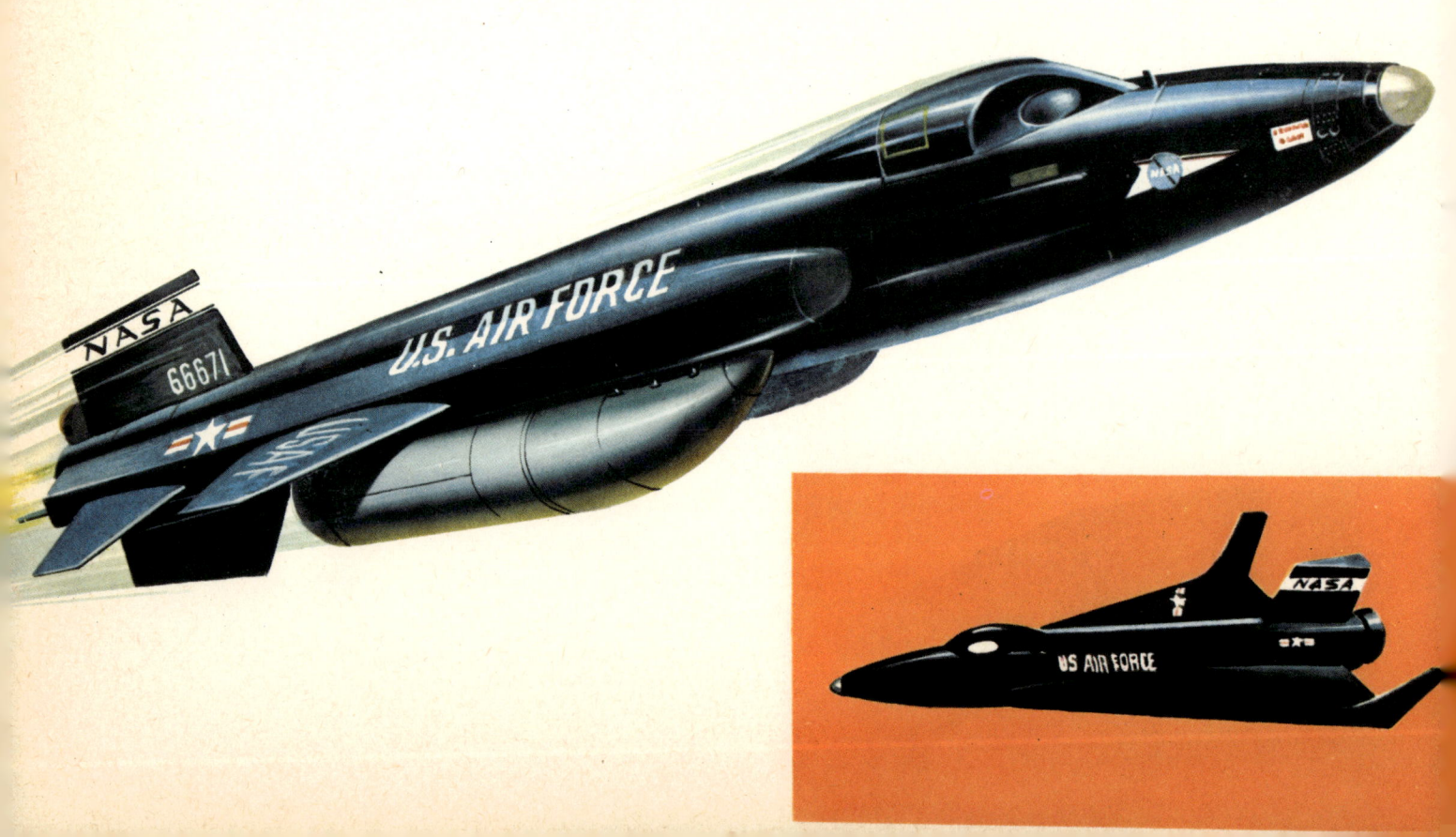

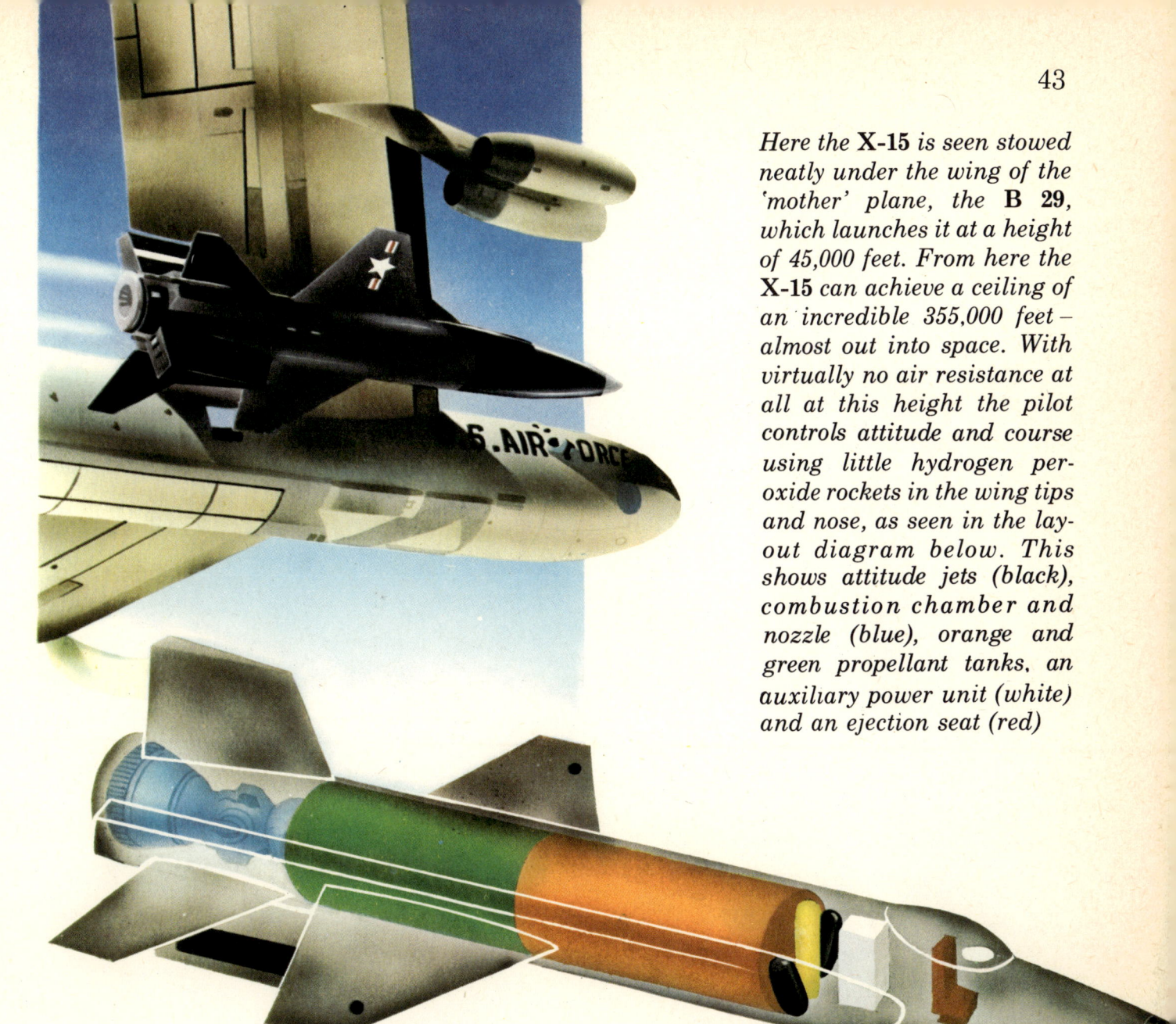

*Here the **X-15** is seen stowed neatly under the wing of the 'mother' plane, the **B 29**, which launches it at a height of 45,000 feet. From here the **X-15** can achieve a ceiling of an incredible 355,000 feet – almost out into space. With virtually no air resistance at all at this height the pilot controls attitude and course using little hydrogen peroxide rockets in the wing tips and nose, as seen in the layout diagram below. This shows attitude jets (black), combustion chamber and nozzle (blue), orange and green propellant tanks, an auxiliary power unit (white) and an ejection seat (red)*

Sooner or later, something not unlike the *X–15* will almost certainly be flying into deep space as a ferry for space stations – perhaps as a rescue plane for spaceships in trouble, or as a tug for transporting sections of building units for orbital station construction.

There is possibly some future in experimenting with the idea of using some version of the design to reverse the pick-a-back roles of the X–plane and the *B–29*, using the small, powerful rocket plane to lift a big carrier plane up to stratospheric heights and supersonic cruising speeds. The little booster plane could then return to base, leaving the large aircraft to fly faster and higher than its own economic engines could ever enable it to do.

Lifting Off

The project which was to have brought the rocket plane and the rocket-powered missile techniques together never actually reached the flying stage. It was designated the *Bell X-20* and was the tool for *Project Dyna-Soar*.

The piloted vehicle was a rocket plane without wings, the fuselage being shaped in a Delta form to provide the necessary lift. Instead of being carried up to operational heights by big bombers, the *X-20* would have made a vertical launch from a conventional space rocket pad, being powered for lift-off by a *Titan* rocket with two additional rocket motors attached to its side.

First the side motors would fire, lift-off and fall away as they burned out. The *Titan II* would then boost the speed and altitude up to 3,500 miles per hour and 250,000 feet. Then the rocket would level out and fall away and the wingless plane fly off on its own rocket power.

Briefly, the principle was that the rocket plane should use all its main propellant in climbing to a height of 150 miles or more, well outside the range of effective atmosphere. It would then go into a steep gliding dive, picking up speed on the way down until it hit firm atmosphere at about 25 miles up. By flattening the dive quickly, the plane could literally bounce off the firm air and shoot up again, repeating the performance in skips and glides of about 2,000 miles each until momentum gave out and a smooth glide down completed the trip which — in theory at least — could have taken it round the world. This novel idea originated in Germany during the war.

The design was thought of as a long-range bomber that could get through any known defences, but the development of guided missiles provided a cheaper

A project which never actually reached the flying stage – the **Dyna-Soar** *Above, an artist's impression of what the* **Dyna-Soar** *would have looked like had it ever taken off. Although the name seems to suggest a prehistoric monster, it was in fact derived from a contraction of 'dynamic soaring'*

and more practical way of delivering a warhead and, later, of intercepting such an attack. Both America and Russia cancelled their skipping bomber projects.

The wingless plane idea has not been abandoned, however, and it has a direct relevance to the next stages in space travel. The current American system of bringing men back from space and dropping them into the ocean to be picked up by helicopters and frogmen is – to put it mildly – a crude way of concluding a remarkable technical achievement. It also takes a lot of time, ships and manpower. The Russian system of landing their bigger craft on firm ground by parachute and retro-rocket is better, but still lands the cosmonauts miles from their true destination.

There is an obvious need for some kind of craft that can fly in space but also land itself like an ordinary aeroplane on an aerodrome.

Wingless planes can do just that, and experimental models have already been built and flown. Called 'lifting body research aircraft', the bullet-nosed, delta shaped prototypes have been taken up by bombers and dropped from high altitudes, diving fast and then flattening out to land at less than 200 m.p.h. under pilot control.

As they are developed, perhaps with some of the know how of jump-jets for ever shorter landing runs, they will be ready to ferry space travellers from their orbiting ships moored to orbiting docks back to earth flying fields.

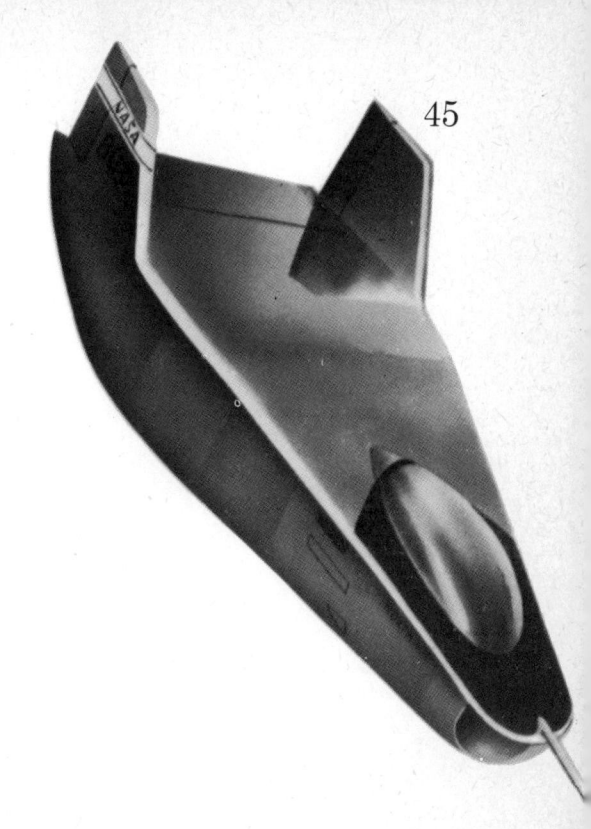

Two examples of the skip bomber gliders. Above, the **Northdrop M2-F2** *and below, the* **Northdrop HL-10** *glider. The principle involved with the skip bomber was that it should be capable of climbing to a height of 150 miles or more, then going into a steep gliding dive until it hit the earth's atmosphere. On flattening the dive, the plane could shoot up again – 'skipping' along on top of the atmosphere belt.*

Rocket Pilots

The hostility of space environment to human life has always been taken for granted. Whether travelling in spacecraft or moving about on the surface of the moon and planets, Man has to envelope himself in a protective shield and carry with him his own life-support systems.

Space-suits, craft, orbiting stations, moon bases and the like are all, in effect, enclosed bits of earth environment transported with the men. They have to provide something to breathe, insulation against heat and cold and some protection against various forms of solar and cosmic radiation. They must also provide something equivalent to atmospheric pressure.

The suits are multi-layered, each layer designed for a specific purpose. Next to the skin is underwear with tiny tubes containing water for cooling purposes. Then comes a lightweight suit designed to slip in and out of the main space suit, then a layer to hold everything together, various insulating layers, and finally an outer suit that is tough enough to stand up to falling around on jagged rocks without tearing. At the neck there is a gas-tight joint for the fitting of the helmet, which has to be linked to the oxygen-supply bottles.

In the early manned flights the astronauts wore the suits all the time, but in 1964 *Voskhod I* carried a three-man crew who removed their suits and travelled in comfort and lightweight clothing for most of the journey. All modern spacecraft are pressurised and air-conditioned, the crews wearing whatever is needed for the jobs in hand. For the first moon landing they wore tough outer suits over the top of the flying suits, discarding the outers before returning to the spacecraft for the homeward journey.

The cabins are a maze of controls and monitoring systems, apart from navigational, observation and photographic equipment. There are indicators for

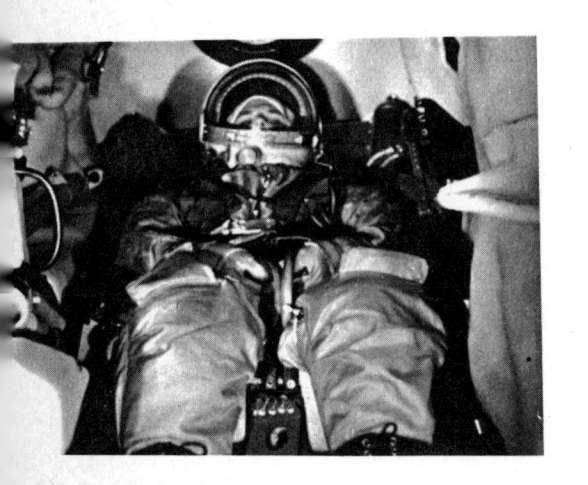

Cosmonaut Yuri Gagarin pictured in the close-fitting interior of **Vostock**. *In early manned space flights both Russian and American spacemen wore their suits all the time. In 1964, however, the three-man crew of* **Voskhod I** *removed their suits and travelled in lightweight clothing for most of the journey*

suit and cabin temperatures, oxygen quantity, air pressure, power supplies and external conditions such as temperature and radiation levels.

Before the actual exploration of space started, there was much speculation about the intensity of solar and cosmic radiation and the extent to which it would prove dangerous to human life in space. There were some people who believed that the hazards were great enough to provide an insuperable barrier to long-range space exploration, but it has since been found that the effects are not a major problem.

Cosmic rays are, of course, reaching us all the time, but they are so filtered by the earth's atmosphere that the effects are not noticeable. The discovery of the Van Allen radiation belts created a new range of possibilities in radiation intensities; if such belts exist near the earth, there may be similar high-intensity fields in the vicinity of other bodies.

Solar radiation at times reaches extremely high levels, but little was known about the frequency or rhythm of such outbreaks. It was for this reason that there was so much cautious probing with instruments and then with animals before the first men went into space. Every astronaut is still being closely watched to see if there have been any long-term effects from radiation, or anything else that can be called a space-sickness, but so far nothing has been discovered to suggest that space is any more unhealthy than the air we breathe down here.

Perhaps the most interesting research experiment into possible genetic effects was in the case of the only woman to fly in space – Valentina Tereshkova – who made 41 orbits in three days in June, 1963.

A N.A.S.A. physician monitors the physical condition of a **Mercury** *astronaut in space*

To support every part of the body during violent accelerations astronauts have moulded couches 'tailored' to their exact measurements

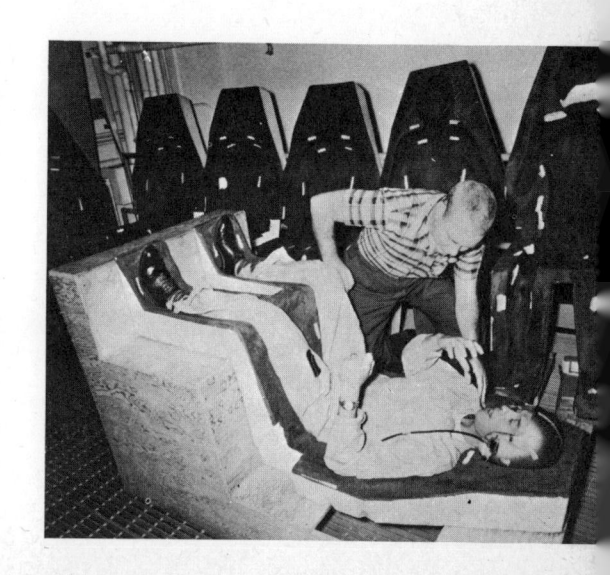

Space Stations

Space stations are already in existence in small sizes. The communications satellites that transmit our radio and television messages round the world, and monitor space radiation and weather movements for us every day, are true space stations. What we usually mean by the term, however, is something more like a celestial railway station – a place where passengers can change craft and obtain rest and refreshment on their journeys. The project of building such a station only requires the allocation of enough money and manpower to become a fact.

The first manned space laboratory was called *Soyuz I* and was piloted into orbit by Vladimir Komarov in April, 1967. It performed satisfactorily over 18 orbits but crashed on landing owing to a faulty parachute, killing its pilot.

The *Soyuz* craft were two-roomed ships designed for intensive study of space conditions, and subsequent flights with docking exercises culminated in a passenger-transfer flight in January, 1969.

The American *Gemini* flights, which included the link-up with the *Agena,* were also space-station experiments in assembling groups of units in space.

Because of the tremendous amount of power needed to get vehicles off the surface of the earth, interest in space stations has grown. The rocketry required to send a ship to change crews on a moon station could place a dozen big, empty ships into orbit, which, when linked up, would make a reasonably comfortable transit hotel and launch pad combined. Quite small, long-lived and refuellable spaceships could operate from such a station,

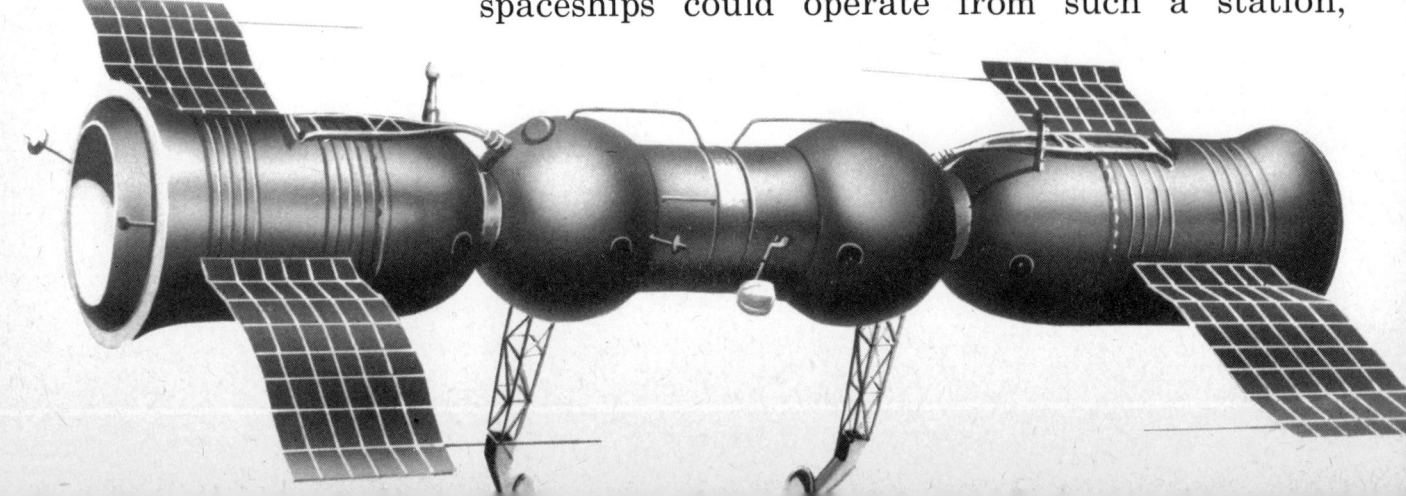

In January 1969 came the first transference of spacemen from one ship to another. The picture shows **Soyuz IV** *and* **V** *linked together in orbit when two of the crew transferred ships for return to earth. A virtual space station prototype,* **Soyuz IV** *and* **V** *each had a laboratory or working area (spherical portions, centre)*

shuttling backwards and forwards to the moon to service permanent observatories there.

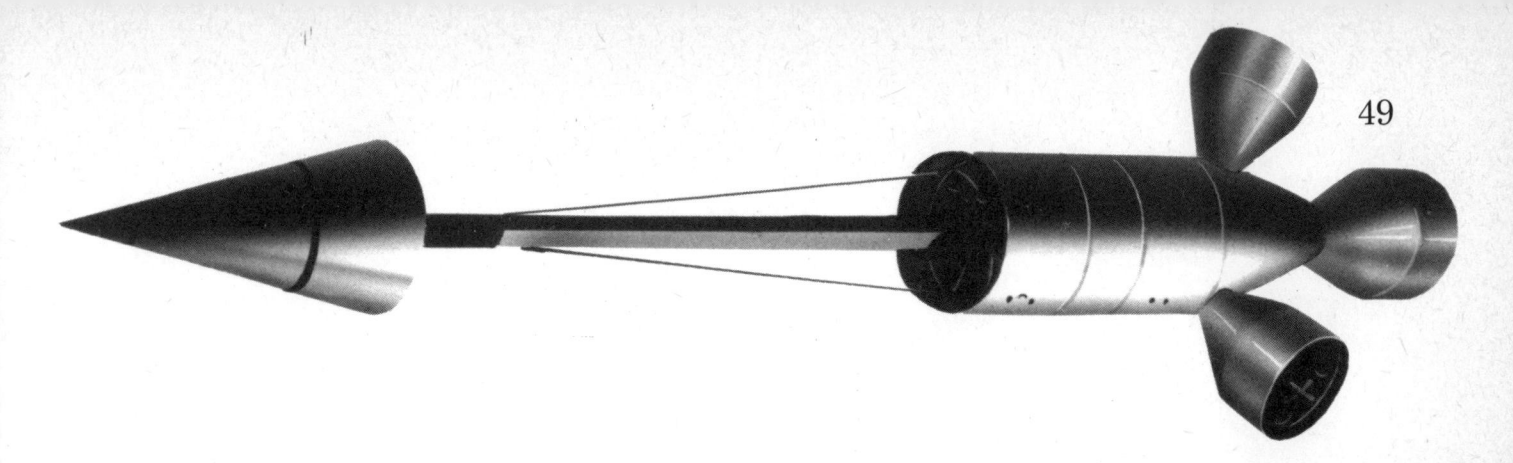

Such a station does not need to be permanently manned. It could stay up for years with an occasional correction of orbit. Fresh supplies, orbiting fuel tanks and other equipment could be sent to its vicinity in unmanned craft, and could literally hang about until a couple of cosmonaut mechanics were sent up to assemble the units.

The station would almost certainly be used as a lifeboat base whenever men were working in space or on the moon. A rescue team could go in at short notice, avoiding the need for a long count-down and the elaborate and expensive equipment required for an earth launch. Space will be much safer once the station is in orbit.

Some time in the future, when manned flights are made into more distant realms of our own solar system or even beyond, it is probable that the take-offs will be made from orbit rather than from earth. It will certainly take the same rocket power to get the long-range spaceship into orbit as it would to get it to Mars, but there are limits to rocket sizes than can be conveniently and economically used. By sending up the Mars ship in sections and assembling it at the space station, smaller, cheaper and easier-to-handle rockets can be employed. The ship itself will be larger and more comfortable for the long trip and, most important of all, it could be tested in space before starting off on its voyage into the unknown.

Probably the next step is the production of a suitable ferry craft that can land on an aerodrome. Once we have this link, the space station becomes invaluable for any kind of future activity.

Space will become much safer for the astronauts the sooner space stations are established. Space scientists envisage them initially as a reasonably comfortable 'hotel' and launch pad combined, from which small space ships could operate. Above is an impression of one of the many versions of large, manned orbital stations now under consideration by the U.S.

The Sputniks

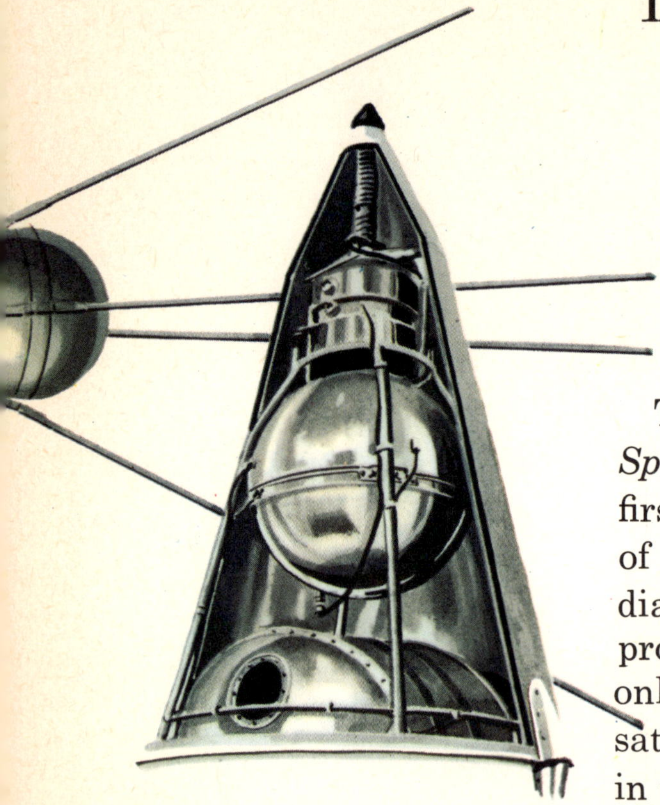

Above, **Sputnik I** *with* **Sputnik II** *inside its nose cone*
Below, **Sputnik III** *with* **Sputnik II** *(red),* **Vanguard** *'grapefruit' test sphere,* **Explorer 1** *and* **Vanguard** *satellites seen on approximately the same scale*

The surprise at the Russian success in launching *Sputnik I* was not wholly because they had got there first; even more amazing was the size and weight of the satellite itself. It was a sphere 23 inches in diameter and weighing 184-lb., compared with the projected *Vanguard* of 20-inches and a weight of only 21-lb. There is no virtue in a big instrumented satellite in itself, the miniaturisation of equipment in the American satellites being technically highly efficient in reducing the payload to be carried. As the weight of the satellite is reflected in the size of the rocket system required to launch it, the Americans had been working with known propellents on rough estimates of 1,000-lb. of rocketry for every one lb. of payload; they had never considered that a satellite of 184-lb. could be a practicable possibility.

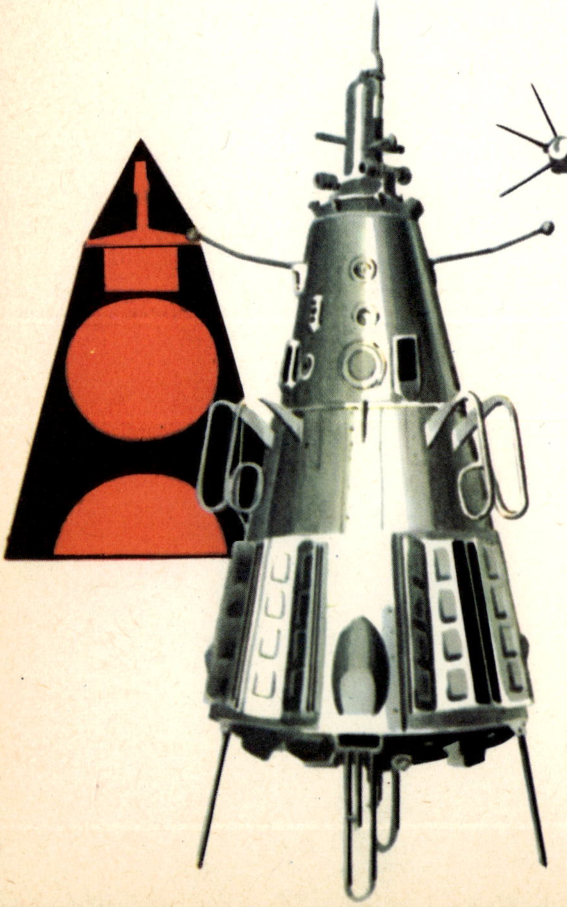

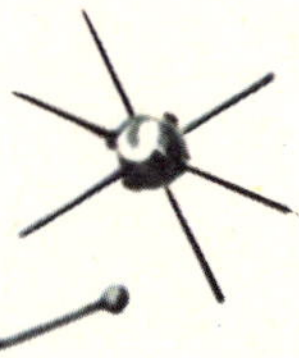

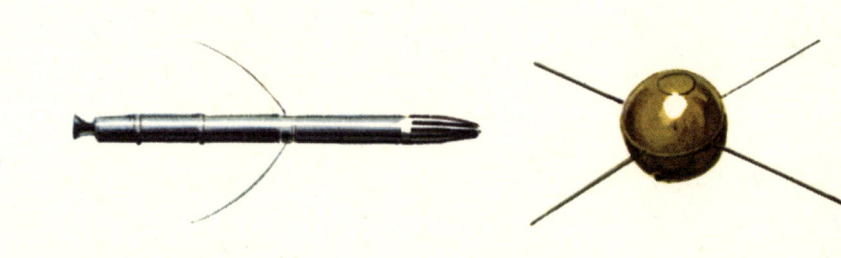

Although the Americans had first overrun the German rocket bases at the end of World War II, and had taken all they could move of the *V–2* weapons and their choice of scientific manpower, it was the Russians who occupied Peenemunde and took over the know-how and manpower left to them. From this start they had worked steadily on the development of large military rockets, and had had considerable success with control and guidance systems. The launching of *Sputnik I* was extremely accurate; its two radio sets functioned well for about three weeks and the 'bleep, bleep' of its tracking signal broadcast the success of Russian technology to the whole world. The satellite travelled in an elliptical orbit with its farthest point (apogee) 588 miles from the earth and its nearest (perigee) 142 miles. This orbit was deliberately planned, as the satellite was designed to test the limits of the atmosphere. Each low pass, however, slowed it a little, until finally it burned up in January, 1958.

Meanwhile, the Americans went ahead with their *Vanguard* project but ran into troubles after the first successful test flight. The second *Vanguard* blew up on its launching pad and the third exploded in the air immediately after launch. Eventually, the programme was modified and a tiny 3½-lb. satellite, the famous 'grapefruit', was put into orbit on March 17th, 1958.

Whereas the Russians had used their big military rockets for the space exploration programme, the Americans had developed in *Viking* and *Vanguard* already available, however, in the *Redstone* and specialised vehicles. Bigger military vehicles were already available, however, in the *Redstone* and *Jupiter* rockets – the latter a mixed assembly of liquid-fuelled *Redstone* base with two tiers of solid-fuel rockets above it, then a final-stage, single solid-fuel rocket designed to spin on separation for directional control. With this vehicle they launched *Explorer I* on January 31st, 1958.

But by this time the Russians had scored more major successes. The first living creature – a dog called Laika – went into space on November 3rd, 1957, with full life-support systems and scientific instruments weighing nearly half a ton. The rocket power required for this *Sputnik II* launching staggered the American engineers, but more was to come. In May, 1958, *Sputnik III* went into orbit. A flying laboratory, packed with instruments, transmitters and batteries, it weighed 2,926-lb. and was in the form of a conical capsule 11-feet 7-inches long. It seemed that the 100-ton space rocket was already a reality.

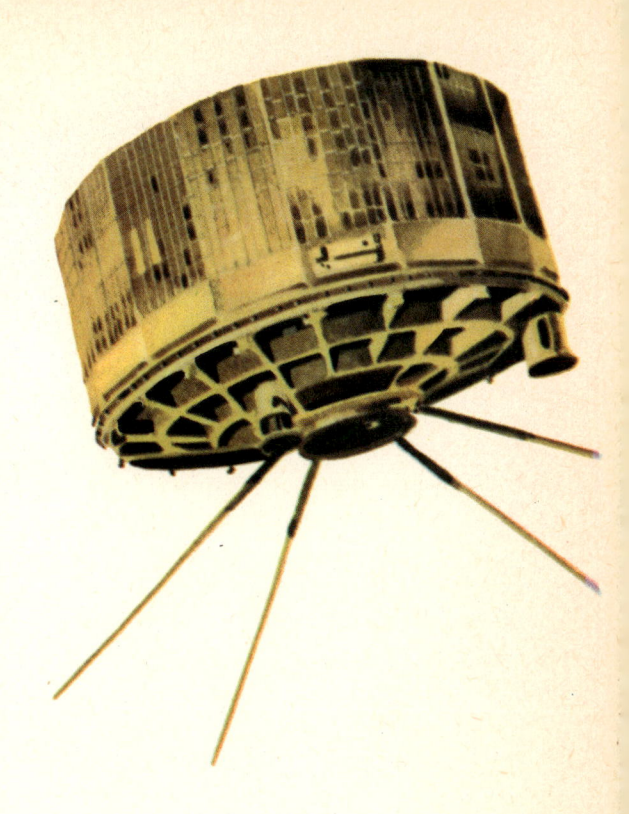

Since **Sputnik I** *scores of satellites have been put into orbit for various purposes. Typical are* **Tiros 1** *(above) the American weather satellite and the French* **'Diapason'** *(below) a geodesic satellite*

Mariner Space Probes

Mariner 2 *(launched August 1962) reconnoitering Venus. It travelled in a wide arc around the sun and passed close enough to Venus to be influenced by the planet's gravity force. Space probes for deep exploration are strange looking craft with large wing-like sections that absorb solar radiation to power their batteries. They carry instruments to observe and transmit information on magnetic fields, cosmic rays, solar winds and micro-meteoroids (space-borne dust)*

Once the main rockets had been developed to the point where they could send men and materials to the moon, they were already powerful enough to go anywhere in the universe. Outside the pull of earth gravity no extra power is needed to travel in space, and future developments in space rocketry will have to be in the direction of greater flexibility and control by radio over immense distances, and by automatic reaction to sensor-supplied information.

This is because the time taken for radio waves to send information back to earth, digest it and send out guidance instructions can be too long to be useful. The long-range space probe must be able to make its own adjustments to meet variations in magnetic or gravitational interference or to avoid collisions with meteoroids. Rocket motors that can be switched on for a fraction of a second to adjust course or speed have already been developed, for example, in the British *Skynet* communications satellite. These techniques will have to be applied to big drive rockets and retro-rockets for inter-planetary and inter-stellar travel.

For the moment, however, the interest in sending probes to the nearer planets of our solar system lies more in the development of the probes themselves than in the rocketry to drive them. Mars and Venus have already been examined by man-made probes – themselves ingeniously-designed flying observatories with television transmitters.

Mariner 2 was despatched to Venus on August 27th, 1962. Venus, said *Mariner 2* firmly, has a

*The Soviet **Venus** probe (right) a version of which landed on the planet in 1966. It was some four times the size of the U.S. **Mariner** probe.*

surface temperature of 400°C and is under a cloud of steam several miles thick.

The Russians aimed much larger spacecraft at Venus – four times the size of the 575-lb. *Mariner*. After several attempts they landed their *Venus 3* on the planet's surface on March 1st, 1966, and on October 18th in the following year they parachute-landed an instrumented capsule from *Venus 4*.

With the same craft and rockets, both countries made a reconnaissance of Mars. *Mariner 4* was launched on October 28th, 1964, and proved the long-range possibilities of navigational control by travelling 325,000,000 miles in 228 days to send back pictures at a range of 5,700 miles from Mars. They showed no indication that the planet was inhabited. The surface was as barren and inhospitable as that of the moon.

Just as the Venus probes discounted the possibility of living beings on that planet, so *Mariner* wrote off the existence of Martians. Perhaps more surprisingly, the observations indicated that the planet has neither magnetic fields nor radiation belts. There is obviously much more to be learned about Mars, but technically the way forward is already planned and charted.

In space where there is no atmosphere, the streamlining of spacecraft – so popular in science fiction – is not necessary. An important function of the early space probes was the information collated about meteorite collisions (registered on the large wing panels) in assessing whether they would endanger later flights – especially manned ones.

*Below is the giant **Pegasus** probe, named after the winged horse of mythology.*

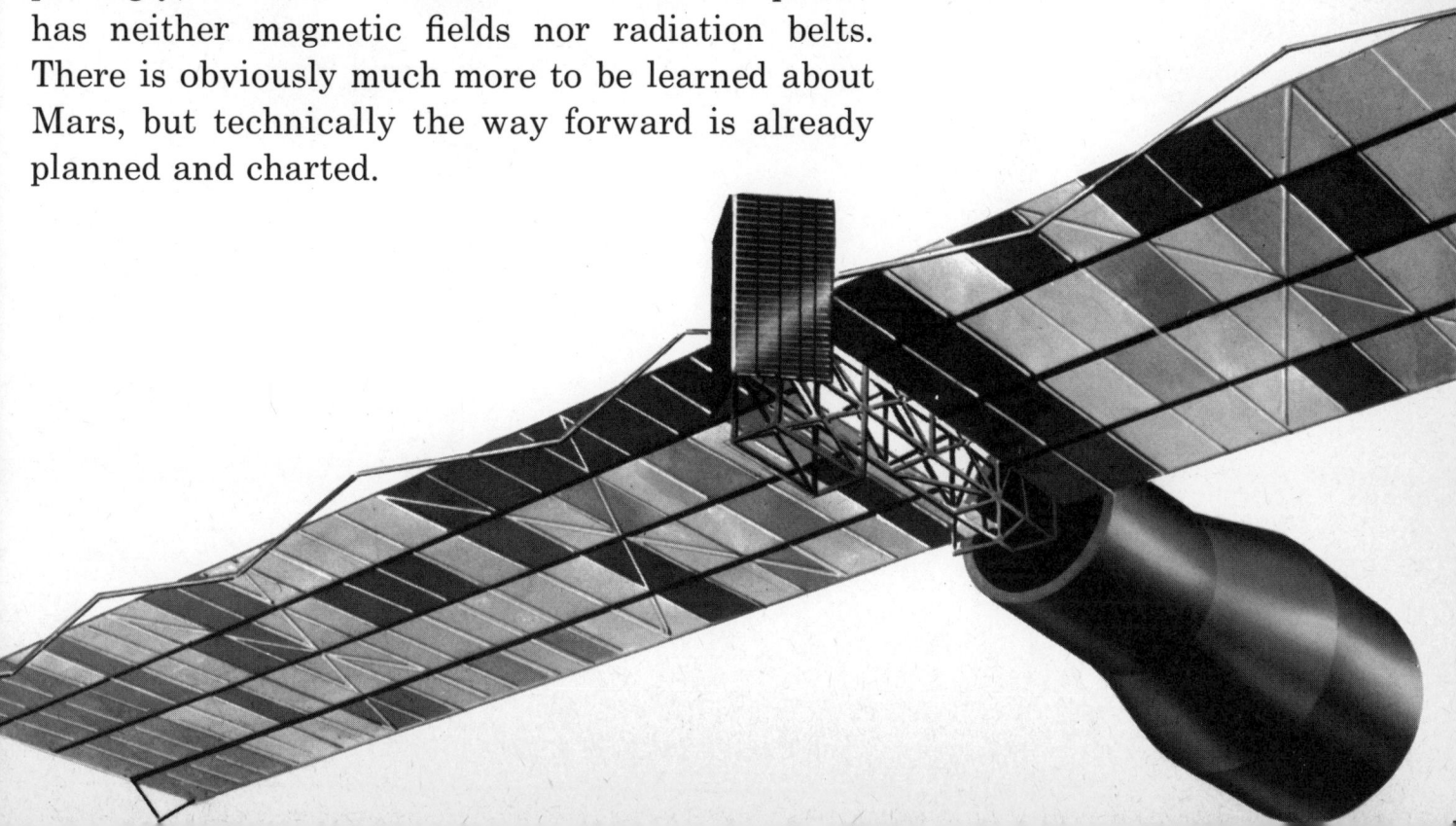

Mariner 4

As well as television photography and its transmission back to earth, **Mariner 4** *was designed to make eight different observations of the planet Mars, magnetic field survey, detecting and measuring cosmic radiation and cosmic dust, the counting of photo electron and alpha particles, measuring the solar wind and establishing the depth and intensity of the Martian atmosphere by measuring radio emissions. Although eventually highly successful almost everything went wrong in the initial construction of* **Mariner 4**

Space engineers must not be disheartened by adversity. So much of what they are using is designed without any previous background of experience that failures must inevitably be frequent.

Time is always a factor in interplanetary flights; they can only take place when the planet is in the right sector of its orbit relative to that of the earth. In the case of Mars, the orbits coincide at 25-month intervals and the available time for launching is less than one month each time round. *Mariner 3,* launched at the beginning of this period, failed to jettison its shroud. Consequently the solar batteries

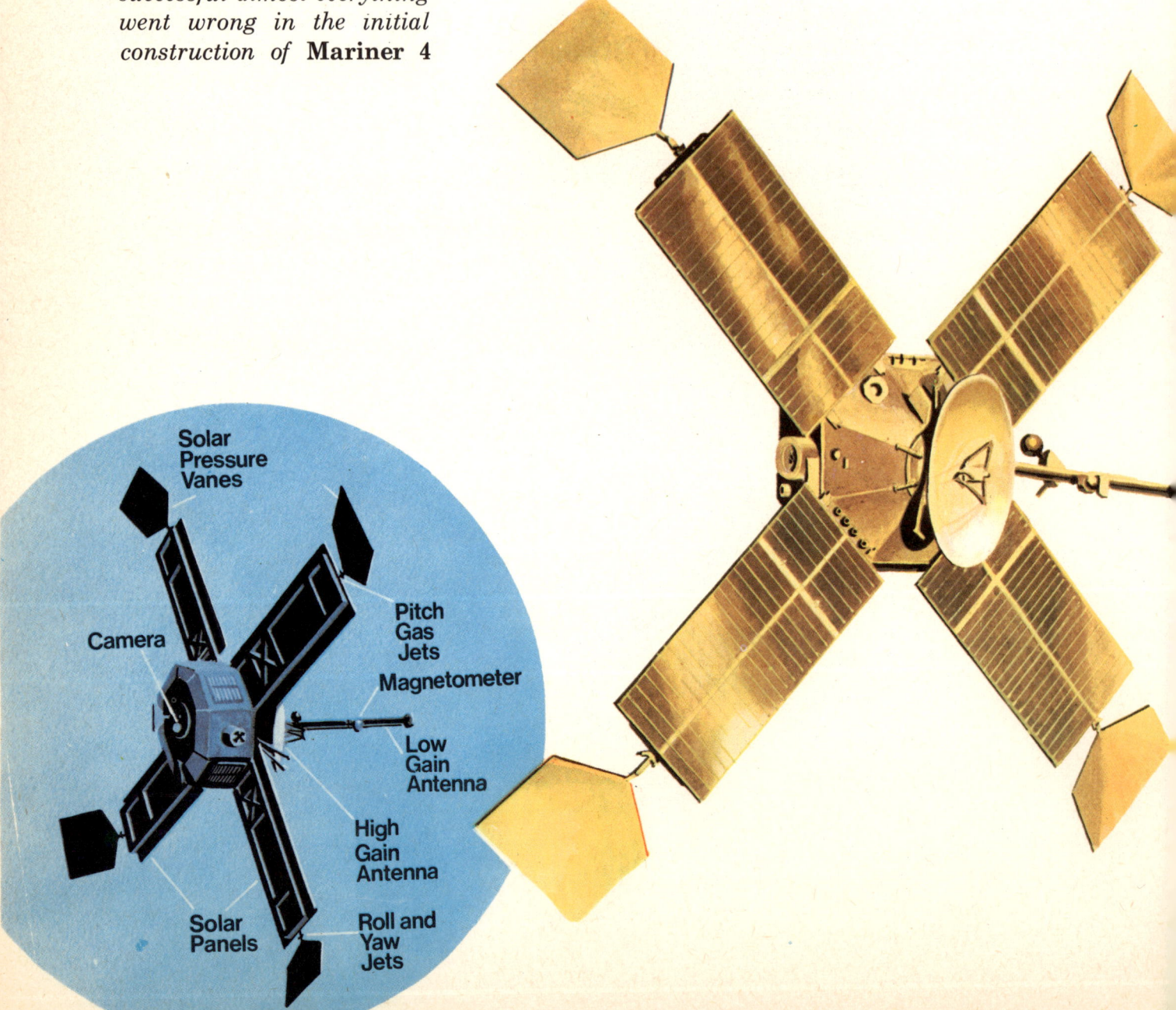

*The **Atlas Agena** two stage rocket (used as a launching vehicle for Mariner 4) which performed perfectly to despatch the spacecraft on its 228 day journey to Mars*

could not operate and the 290-lb. weight of the shroud held the speed too low for its planned trajectory.

Fortunately, a spare rocket vehicle and spacecraft had been prepared. The designers set to work to design and make a new shroud and fit it to *Mariner 4*. They succeeded in 23 days, leaving just four days to spare. Then it was found that the new shroud was 47-lb. heavier than the first one, so some agonising decisions had to be made about what equipment must be taken out of the craft, and circuits modified accordingly.

Count-down began on November 27th, 1964, but trouble was experienced in the radio control system and the launch was put off for another day. The launch, on the morning of the 28th, was successful.

However, all was not yet well. The navigational system was designed to enable the craft's inertial guidance device to lock on to the sun on one axis and then 'roll and search' until it locked on to the bright star Canopus. Naturally, a spacecraft cannot tell one star from another and can select only on the intensity of the stars within its arc of search.

What had not been foreseen was that small pieces of debris from the second stage would be floating around the craft and glinting brightly in the sunlight. These particles confused the craft and it continued its 'roll and search' manoeuvres until ground control locked it on to Canopus and cut out the search circuits altogether.

The television camera stored its 70 seconds of photography on tape and then played it back very slowly, taking eight hours per picture to give high definition. There were 40,000 dots per picture in 64 shades of grey from white to black.

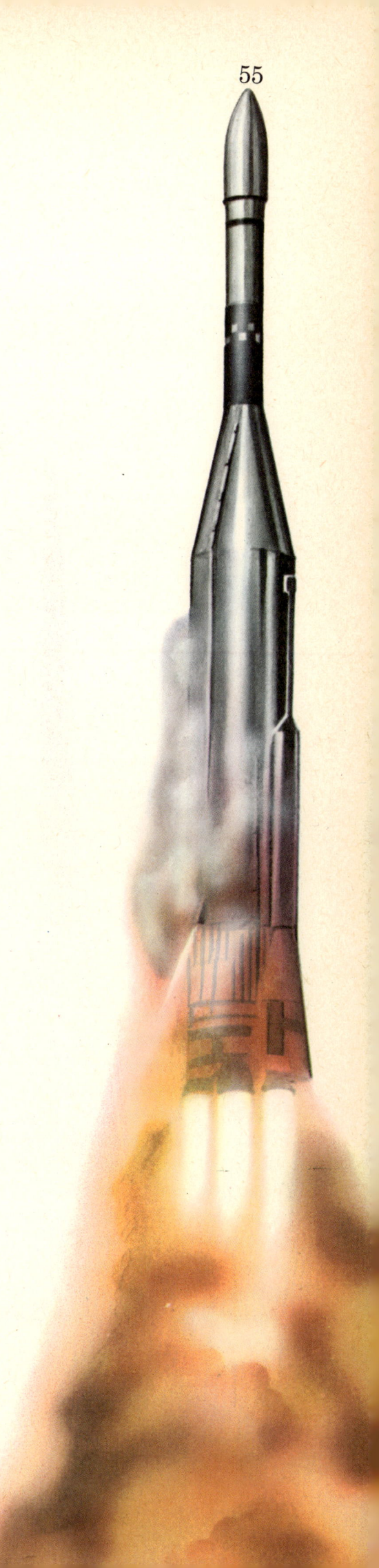

Titan, Delta, Agena

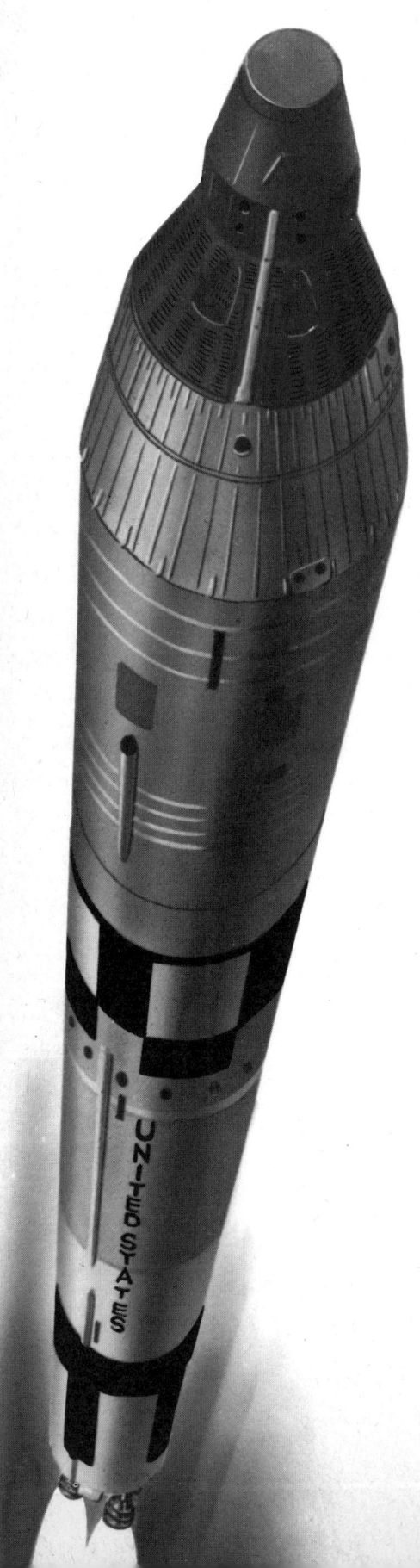

*The **Titan** missile adapted as a launcher for the Gemini capsule*

Limits of performance were continuously extended and new rockets constantly designed for new tasks during the first decade of the space age.

By the early '60s, however, the shape of things to come was more clearly measurable and rockets could be designed with relatively long-term requirements in view. With the success of *Atlas,* the American programme settled down to the use of a group of rocket vehicles which could be teamed up in stages to meet the requirements of any particular launching project.

Atlas was closely followed by the *Titan* series – larger but simpler, with a conventional series-burning two-stage system.

Titan II was supplemented, but not replaced, by *Titan III*. This vehicle used the basic *Titan II* liquid-fuelled main rocket with a pair of smaller solid-fuelled boosters strapped to its sides, and fluid injection steering. It makes a powerful launching vehicle for heavy lifts. First the boosters fall away, then the main rocket, leaving the second stage and payload to be manoeuvred in space with full fuel stocks.

At its first launch on June 19th, 1965, *Titan III* weighed 1,419,000 lb. and carried a payload of 21,000 lb., which was by far the heaviest load then sent up by the Americans.

Delta rockets made their appearance as power units for intercepting enemy bombers. They were virtually unmanned fighter aircraft, but were quickly adapted by the space administration and used as launching vehicles for the *Explorer* series of satellites. They were later adapted as second stages and mounted on *Titan* boosters, thus leaving the military field for serious space research.

Agena, too, is a second-stage rocket but it is designed to operate in space rather simply to get there. It was an *Agena* on top of an *Atlas* that carried the *Ranger* moon probes into orbit, and an *Agena*

*The basic **Agena** rocket (top) designed specifically to operate in space, shown with the **Agena** amended to target vehicle.*

*Below the **Delta** three stage launch vehicle with the U.K. Ariel satellite atop as payload*

on *Titan II* that opened the *Gemini* manned-spacecraft programme.

An adaptable tool, it is liquid-fuelled and controllable from the ground or the spacecraft itself. Its engines can be switched on and off as required, making possible the docking manoeuvres and space walks of the astronauts.

For the *Gemini 8, 9* and *10* flights – which were designed to try out docking and space-walking techniques – the *Agena* rocket sections were fired into orbit on their own by *Atlas* boosters, followed a couple of hours later by the *Titan*-powered *Gemini* spacecraft. On the first mission, the spacecraft developed a spin and had to abandon the rocket. With *Gemini 9* the *Agena* was lost when the upper stage of the carrier misfired. But with the *Gemini 10* flight all went well. The *Atlas* fired the *Agena* into orbit and two hours later the spacecraft was launched on a *Titan II* and docked with it.

On docking, the astronauts started up the *Agena's* engines and used it to push themselves to an apogee of 475 miles – farther in space than any human beings had ever been before.

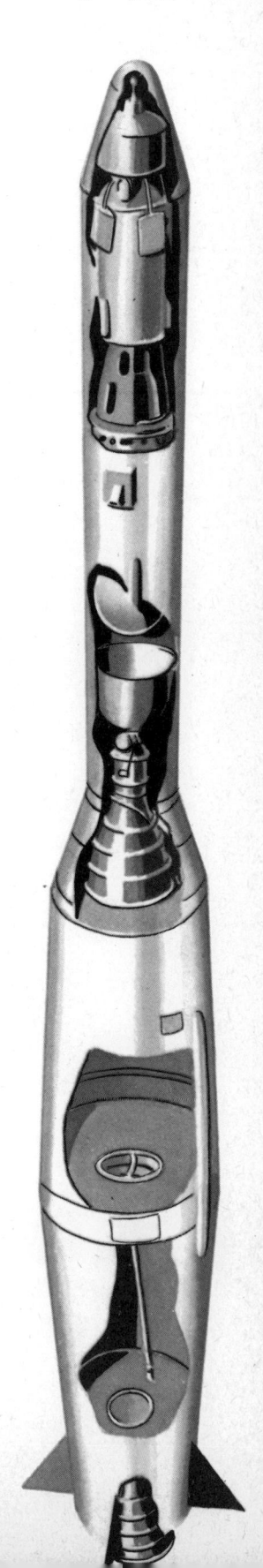

The Mercury Project

Mercury was the name of the American project for putting men into space, but the first passenger to travel in a *Mercury* spacecraft was a chimpanzee called Ham. On January 31st, 1961, Ham made a sub-orbital trip to a height of 155 miles and splashed down safely.

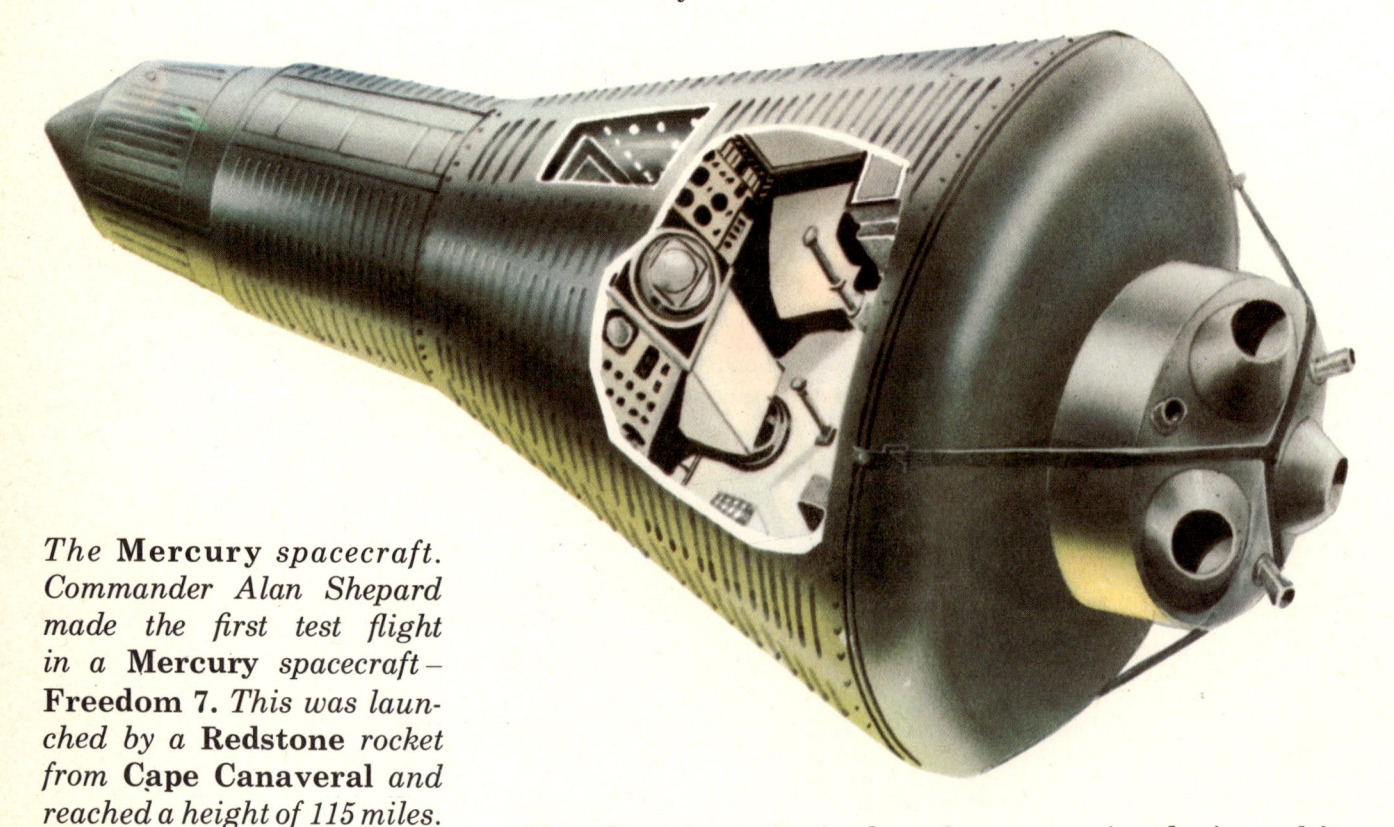

*The **Mercury** spacecraft. Commander Alan Shepard made the first test flight in a **Mercury** spacecraft – **Freedom 7**. This was launched by a **Redstone** rocket from **Cape Canaveral** and reached a height of 115 miles. Shepard made a parachute descent into the sea in the capsule and was successfully recovered*

The Russians had already put animals in orbit, and on April 12th that year they put the first man into space – Major Gagarin – who completed a single orbit inside the capsule *Vostock I* and landed safely. NASA (National Aeronautics and Space Administration) had laid on a programme of sub-orbital flights and refused to be pressured into changing schedules and taking risks, to catch up with the Russians.

In May, Commander Alan Shepard and in July Captain Virgil Grissom, made successful test flights in *Mercury* spacecraft. Repeat sub-orbital flights were made, including another with a chimpanzee as 'pilot', and the test programme was completed by the end of that year.

In February, 1961, the first American went into orbit round the earth; Lt.-Colonel John Glenn of the U.S. Marine Corps made a three-orbit flight in a *Mercury* craft called *Friendship 7* which was powered by an *Atlas* rocket.

Launch and navigation during the flight went well, but there was trouble with the automatic control system during the re-entry phase, Colonel Glenn having to bring the capsule down on its retro-rockets by manual control. The splash-down was perfect and on target, so the incident helped rather than hindered the research.

The three-orbit flight was repeated on May 24th, 1962, by Lt-Commander Scott Carpenter. Again the flight went well but the astronaut had some difficulties on the splash-down and had to eject from the capsule in the sea. Five months later, Commander Walter Schirra made a six-orbit flight on October 3rd which went without a hitch. Finally, on the 15th and 16th May, 1963, Major Gordon Cooper made a 22-orbit flight which covered 583,469 miles – far enough to make a trip to the moon and back – making a planned manual descent with pinpoint accuracy.

By the conclusion of the *Mercury* project, America had six astronauts who had travelled in space, a tried and tested system of ground control and inter-communication, and a proven design of spacecraft with all its instrumentation and life-support systems operating efficiently and reliably. The programme did, in fact, do everything it had set out to do, and make the idea of space travel real and acceptable to government and public alike.

The limits imposed by the available rockets, *Redstone* and *Atlas*, had kept the size and weight of the *Mercury* capsules down to about 2,000-lb. But the American know-how in the miniaturisation of instruments had enabled a very compact design of ship to be built. It was clear, however, that the next phase in the space programme would need both bigger ships and bigger rockets to launch them, and these were forthcoming for the next project – the two-man satellite *Gemini*.

Below, an **Atlas** *rocket, carrying the* **Mercury** *space capsule* **Friendship 7** *with Lt.-Colonel John Glenn inside, blasts off the launching pad at* **Cape Canaveral,** *February 20th, 1961*

Russian Cosmonaut Programme

It was the Russian lead in the size of booster rockets that made their spaceships and space programme so very different from that of the Americans. The huge, multi-stage rocket assembly that put Major Gagarin into orbit in *Vostock I* had already proved that it could put a 4½-ton capsule into orbit. *Sputnik V* was such a ship, and it had been put into orbit and successfully recovered in August, 1960, with a 'crew' of two dogs, twelve mice, insects, plants and cultured microbes.

When the *Vostock* was shown to the world in 1967 it was seen just how great the differences between the two systems had been. The launching rocket of the Russian craft was nearly 125-feet tall and consisted of a two-stage main core with four boosters grouped round the lower half, all being liquid fuelled. There were four primary nozzles and two verniers on each of the booster units, and four primaries and four verniers on the main first stage.

With the amount of power available, the capsule was not restricted in size and weight. *Vostock I* was 10,418-lb. loaded and the spherical capsule was a simple and roomy affair compared with the *Mercury* craft.

The pilot lay on an ejector seat (not used on the flight), and could reach all controls without movement. Food, water, recording tape, television camera, radio, sanitary system and manual controls for the retro-rockets and landing parachute were all pro-

The first woman in space – cosmonaut Valentina Tereskova – flew a successful mission in June 1963

*First shown to the world in 1967, the huge **Vostock** launcher (right) was nearly 125 feet tall with four liquid-fuelled boosters. Its 32 rocket chambers fired sumultaneously to produce a massive take-off thrust of 1,000,000 lbs. With this power at their disposal the Russians were able to launch unexpectedly large capsules compared with the Americans. **Vostock I** was a spacious craft weighing 10,418 lbs loaded*

vided, there appearing to have been no attempt to save weight or space by extensive miniaturisation as on the American pattern.

Before America had a man in orbit, Gagarin had orbited in *Vostock I* and Titov had circled the world all day in *Vostock II*. On August 11/12th, Nikolayev in *Vostock III* and Popovich in *Vostock IV* had orbited together and manoeuvred their craft to within three miles of each other. In June, 1963, the first woman cosmonaut – Valentina Tereshkova – went into space. She also had an escort in close company, in Valery Bykovsky in *Vostock V*. On October 12th, 1964, a new and even larger spaceship appeared in the sky – *Voskhod I*. It had a three-man crew of whom only Vladimir Komarov was a pilot. The other two were an air force doctor named Boris Yegorov and a civilian scientist, Konstantin Feoktistov. The entire crew took off their space-suits and travelled through most of the flight in ordinary lightweight clothing. The experiment proved successful and set the pattern for future manned flights.

Except for Gagarin in *Vostock I*, all previous Russian cosmonauts had used ejector seats and parachutes to land. Using air brakes, a new design of parachute and retro-rockets, *Voskhod I* landed with its crew inside.

On March 18th, 1965, *Voskhod II* – carrying Colonel Pavel Belyayev and Lt.-Colonel Aleksei Leonov – was launched by a new rocket with a thrust of 1,430,000-lb. – bigger than anything used before. Another 'first' was scored when Leonov left the craft to walk in space.

A spherical capsule of 7 feet 6 inches in diameter, the **Vostock** *spaceship (left) was equipped with a heavy heatshield which acted as a gravity weight in bringing it down right side up on landing. All controls were within easy reach without undue movement by the pilot and by comparison with the current U.S. counterparts was luxuriously fitted out*

Gemini

On March 23rd 1965 five days after Leonov's space walk, the *Gemini III* spacecraft was launched by a *Titan II* rocket carrying Virgil Grissom – the first man to go into space a second time – and John Young. Their task was to test the craft for manoeuvring ability in changing plane and height of orbit.

The American *Gemini* programme was based on enlarged and modified versions of the *Mercury* craft and was intended to try out techniques of docking with other satellites in space.

On June 3rd, James McDivitt and Edward White went into orbit in *Gemini IV*, and White walked in space. For the first time the space-walker used power for independent flight in the form of a pack of three mini-rocket motors running on hydrazine and water and producing a thrust of about 2-lb. The idea worked well and White was able to work his way round the craft to prove the practicability of repair work or modification of aerials and so on under space conditions. *Gemini IV* also had the task of making rendezvous and keeping station with the burned-out second stage of its launching rocket, but the rocket went astray.

Gemini V was more successful and kept station with its *Titan* second stage for a considerable part of its 119-orbit, eight-day flight, with Gordon Cooper – making his second orbital flight – and Charles Conrad as crew. But the big event came on December 4th, when *Gemini VII* took off with Frank Borman and James Lovell on the longest flight yet attempted. After eleven days in orbit they were met by *Gemini VI*, crewed by Walter Schirra and Thomas Stafford. The sister ships came within inches of each other and practised formation flying and manoeuvring for four hours.

Gemini VI returned to earth next day and tested new ground-guidance equipment on the way down. *Gemini VII* went on to cover a total of 105 orbits in two weeks – a record time in space.

Docking would obviously be the next move, and the Americans decided to make it a linking-up between a manned craft and an *Agena* 'space tug' separately launched. The *Agena* set off on March 16th, 1966, and was followed by Neil Armstrong and David Scott in *Gemini VIII*. They docked successfully but almost immediately one of the *Gemini's* thrusters jammed open and put the craft into a spin. The crew disengaged from the *Agena* and came down safely on emergency control – proving that things could go wrong in space without being fatal.

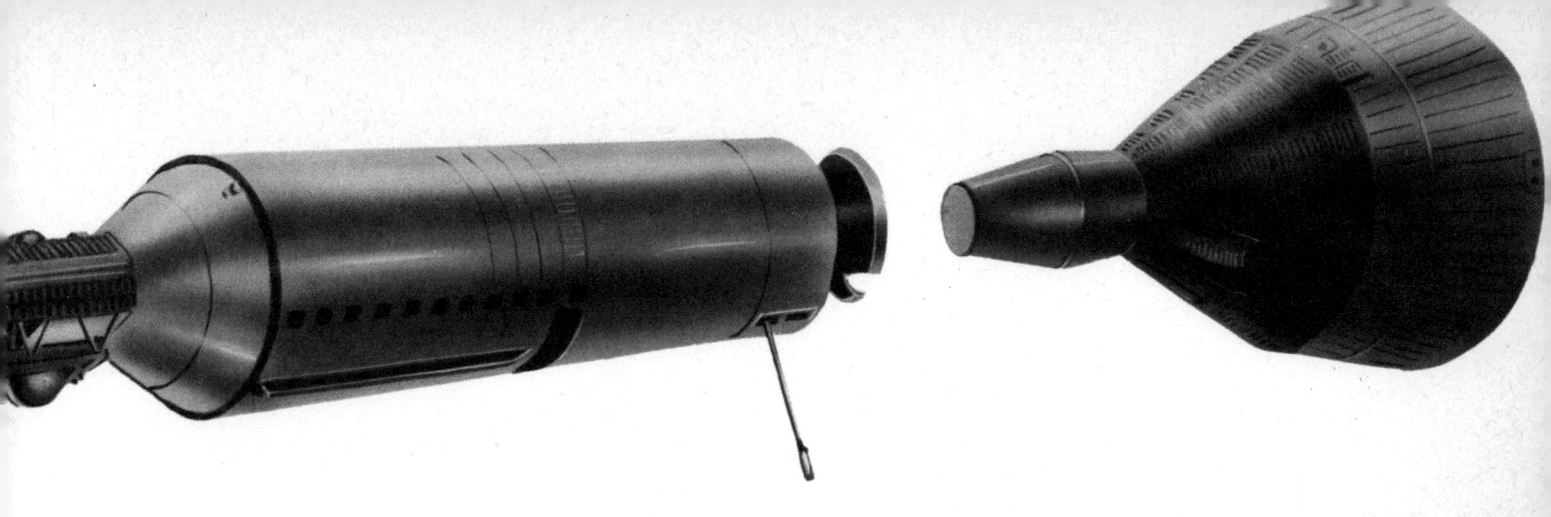

Gemini IX made another attempt but was foiled by jammed fairings, which Eugene Cernan could not free. However, he put in some space walk practice and the craft returned safely.

Gemini X – crewed by John Young and Michael Collins – docked first with the *Agena 10* satellite, then used the *Agena's* engine to rendezvous with *Agena 8*, which was still in orbit after the first docking experiment with *Gemini VIII*. Collins used the mini-rocket pack to go over to the *Agena* and back.

The next flight was by *Gemini XI* on September 12th, with Charles Conrad and Richard Gordon as crew. They met up with *Agena 11* and used its engine to set up a new orbit apogee level for a manned spaceflight of 850 miles above the earth. Gordon worked in space for 44 minutes.

On the last *Gemini* flight, Edward Aldrin spent $5\frac{1}{2}$ hours outside the spacecraft. He and James Lovell put in 59 orbits and brought the *Gemini* project to a satisfactory conclusion on November 15th, 1966. By this time America had a large force of experienced astronauts and had tested all her space equipment thoroughly.

Increasingly successful attempts at space docking were undertaken by the Americans in 1966. In September of that year astronauts Conrad and Gordon in **Gemini XI** *docked with the* **Agena** *spacecraft. The picture shows the* **Gemini** *capsule about to dock with the* **Agena** *target vehicle*

Getting the Message

Rocket vehicles are not an end in themselves, of course. They are simply the means for putting into orbit satellites that will observe, record and transmit to earth the effects of natural phenomena that scientists wish to study.

A typical instrumentation package in an earth satellite would contain a solar cell battery, charged by sunlight, and possibly an auxiliary battery to continue observation and transmission while the satellite is in the shadow of the earth. There would also be an ion chamber to detect ultra-violet radiation, cosmic ray counters, photographic equipment and spectrum-analysis prisms.

Thermosistor strips measure the variable outside skin temperature of the satellite during orbit. There is also an erosion gauge which measures cumulative abrasion by dust – or, in the scientists' terms, micro-meteorites. The knowledge thus gained will be vital when the time comes to build space vessels for very long journeys. Another invaluable device is a recording tape, which records the frequency and weight of impact of larger particles of meteoric origin. An amplifier receives the signals from skin microphones and passes them to the tape for storage and later transmission.

All the information picked up by the various sensors has to be recorded and then coded into a

The antennae site at the 'Distant Space Communications Centre' of the U.S.S.R. Academy of Sciences

Part of the Russian tracking and receiving station where messages transmitted by spacecraft are retaped and decoded.

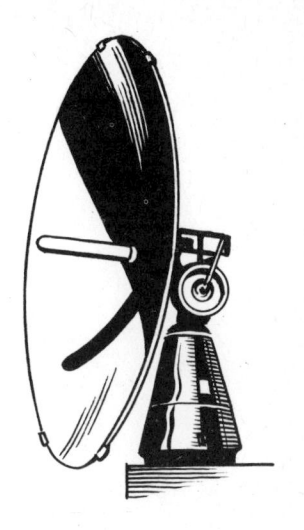

system of radio wave transmissions that can be sent back to earth. These Telemetry Coding Systems are the most complicated electronic instruments in the satellites.

The atmosphere of the earth is a remarkable insulator. It effectively prevents gamma and X-rays from reaching its surface. If this were not so, life would be insupportable here. But the atmosphere also limits and bends light rays, so that visual inspection of the heavens from earth – even with the most powerful telescopes ever made – is limited in its range and value.

From a satellite operating outside the atmosphere, however, a simple, small lens camera or telescope can see way out among the stars. Every satellite is an astronomical observatory far more efficient than, for example, Mount Palomar with its huge 200-inch telescope. Fortunately, radio waves do get through the atmosphere and so the observations of the satellites are transmitted back to earth.

Apart from weapons, both America and Russia use satellites as sophisticated spies to photograph military and naval installations, study radar developments and even spy on each other's satellites. Because the element of surprise is almost eliminated by this kind of observation, the risk of war preparations being pushed to dangerous limits is reduced. The satellite as a super spy may itself be a major contributor to world peace.

Both the United States and Russia maintain networks of stations around the world to track and communicate with spacecraft. They include a number of tracking ships, above left, which fill in the gaps in the land-based stations. The usual type of antenna used is dish-shaped. Another type is shown below.

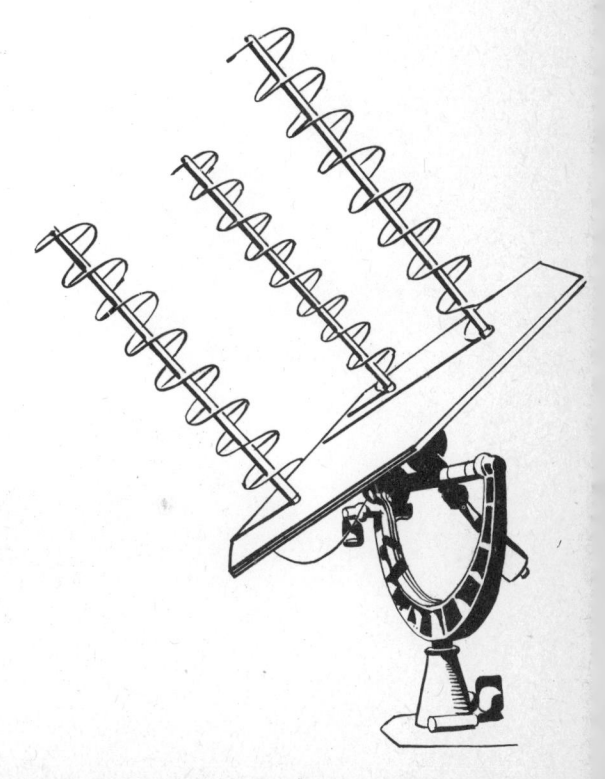

Space probe – Moon

'Reaching for the moon' has been the phrase used to describe Man's boundless ambition. Now that the moon has been reached, the ultimate goal has been changed to the planets and even the stars. The moon is the earth's only satellite, the nearest thing to us in space, so for the study of this earth – its weather, ecological changes, its place in cosmology – the moon would be an immensely valuable observatory. With no distorting air, radiation belts, temperature and humidity factors to obstruct it, a moon-based observatory would not require huge, 200-inch telescopes to study the heavens visually; radio and radar transmission and reception would be greatly improved; and laser beam surveys would be minutely accurate over light years of inter-stellar distance. We need to use the moon as a stepping stone to Outer Space.

From the launching of *Sputnik I* to the first moon probe attempt was less than a year, though the *Thor-Able* rocket failed to reach escape velocity and fell back after climbing to a height of 70,000 miles. Soon afterwards the Russians despatched *Luna I*. Despite its massive 796-lb load, the powerful Russian rocket sent the probe all the way. *Luna I* missed the moon by some 4,600 miles, and went into orbit round

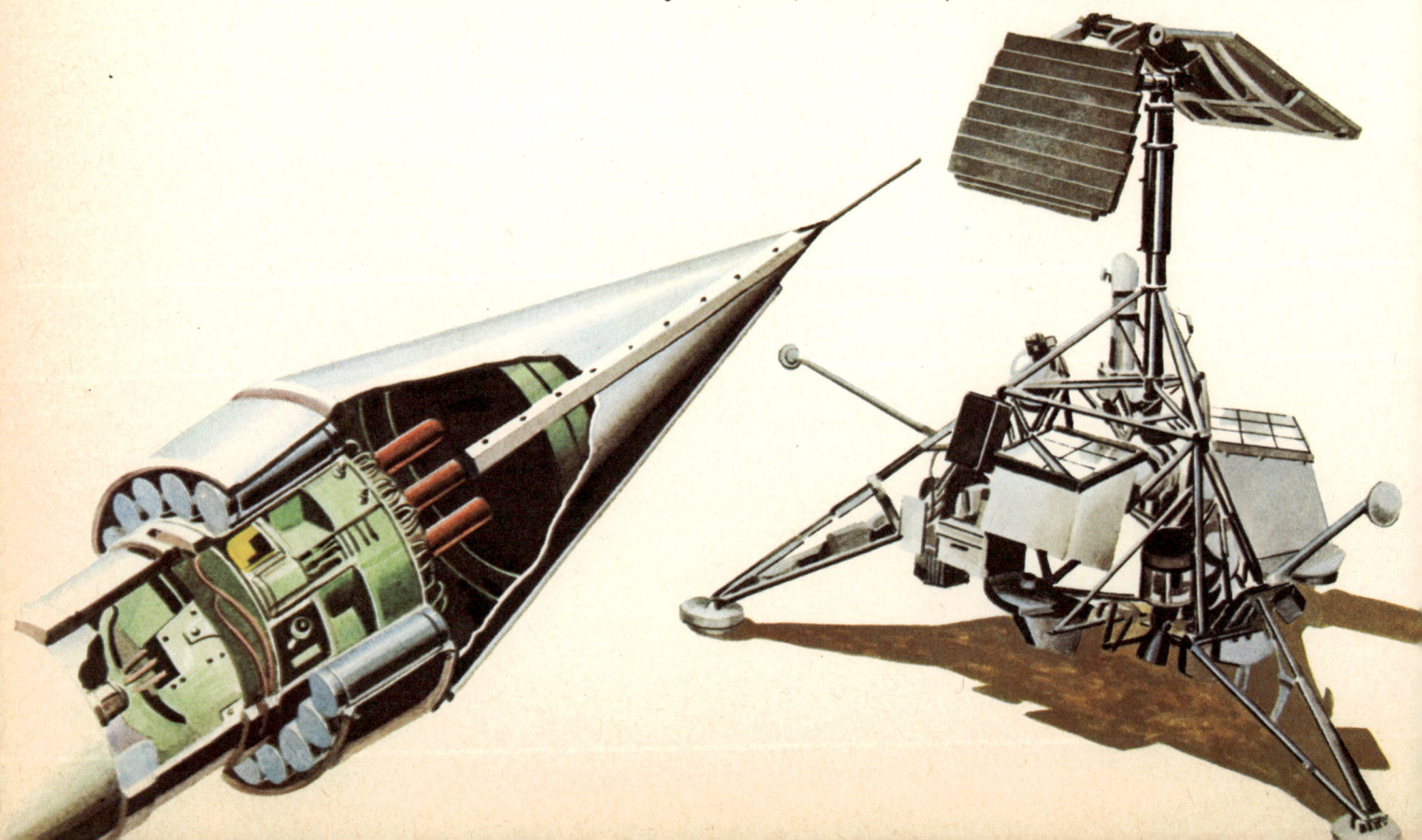

*An early moon probe sent into space by the Americans, **Pioneer IV**. Like the earlier attempt by the Russians this probe missed the moon itself and went into orbit around the sun. It was under two feet in length and this diagram shows the batteries (blue), cosmic ray detectors (red) and transmitter (yellow). The **Surveyor** spacecraft (right) was 10 feet tall and had rocket systems to control landing approach. It was also equipped with solar panel, T.V. cameras and several different kinds of antennae*

the sun. *Pioneer IV* did the same.

Then the Russians scored the first direct hit on the moon on September 14th, 1959, with *Luna II*. It is a wry comment on the importance of national prestige as an incentive in the space race that the payload of the Russian moon probe was nothing more scientific than a load of hammer and sickle badges. And when the Americans were first to land men on the moon, they carried a mini-flag bearing the stars and stripes!

Less than three weeks later, on October 4th, *Luna III* passed right round the moon and sent back the first pictures ever seen of the 'other side' – that part we never see from the earth.

After five attempts to explore the moon's surface photographically by soft-landing ejected instrumented packages just before impact, the Americans settled for sending pictures back to earth by television. *Ranger VII* did this successfully in July, 1964. Later, *Ranger IX* sent pictures that were shown live on domestic television. For the first time we, the people, saw what we were getting for our money.

*The first pictures ever seen of the moon's 'other side' were sent back to earth by the Russian **Luna III** (below) In this diagram the probe is turned to enable its cameras to photograph the moon's surface. The advanced **Luna IX** (below left) had controlled descent ability plus a network of T.V. systems capable of sending remarkably clear pictures back to earth*

Saturn I

The *Saturn* rockets were designed as part of the *Apollo* moon landing project, and for the first time the line of development was laid down from the start. *Saturn IB* was ready for flight by the time *Saturn I* had been tested, and both these were ground-work for *Saturn V*, which would carry the manned capsules to the moon.

After the abandonment of the *Nova* rocket programme, the efforts of the designers were turned more towards greater efficiency than size. *Atlas* and *Titan* were good examples of the new kind of liquid-fuelled rockets. But the moon flight demanded high launching power and the *Saturns* had to be big as well as efficient.

Saturn I was designed to put a one-ton load into orbit. The first stage was a group rocket with a thrust of 1,504,000-lb.; the second stage was a single core giving 90,000-lb. thrust. *Saturn's* real success lay in its utter reliability; all ten flights were completely trouble-free and successful. They included launches of mock-up shells of the *Apollo* capsules containing meteoric detectors.

The specific function of *Saturn IB* was to test the three modules of the *Apollo* craft in orbit – *Command*, *Service* and *Lunar Excursion* – and when the first flight was made on February 26th, 1966, it was a nearly full-scale rehearsal for the time when *Saturn V* would take up the whole projected 40-ton payload. The testing was severe and included low-angle climbs which were designed to find any weaknesses in the structure.

After climbing 37 miles, the first stage blew off on small retro-rockets at a speed of 4,300 m.p.h. and the second stage started burning; then the escape tower was jettisoned and the climb continued to a height of 52 miles and a speed of 15,000 m.p.h. – nearly 1,000 miles from its launching pad. Then, still climbing, the rocket was turned nose down and the *Apollo* craft freed, continuing to climb to a final altitude of 310 miles.

The escape tower that had been jettisoned earlier was designed to release the module containing the the crew from the launcher in case of a first-stage failure. Once the stage had separated, there was no longer any need for it, as the *Service Module* could itself handle any failure of the second stage. The parts that went on climbing on this first *Saturn IB* tests were the *Command Module,* which would be the crew cabin, and the *Service Module,* which had its own engine and provided electrical power. Together but unmanned, these weighed 33,800-lb. The *Lunar Excursion Module* was not carried on the first test.

On the downward journey the reaction control system rockets were fired twice, bringing the speed of the craft up to 18,000 m.p.h. and separating the *Command Module* for its re-entry. The whole manoeuvre proved the efficiency of the ground control and automatic re-entry procedures, as well as that of the *Saturn IB* rocket.

The entire *Saturn IB* programme was designed as a testing and development phase of the *Apollo* moon mission, and all flights were completely successful from the point of view of the rocketry. The last flight of the *IB* in this programme was *Apollo 5*, when the *Lunar Module LM1* was launched from Cape Kennedy on January 22nd, 1968. It was described at the time as only 'a qualified success', as some trouble was experienced with the firing of the ascent and descent engines of the *Module*. But flight capacity had been confirmed, and the way was now clear for the *Saturn V* launchings aimed at moon landing.

All ten flights of the **Saturn** *programme by the Americans were completely successful.* **Saturn IB** *had increased power over its prototype I. The eight engines of the first stage gave a thrust output of 1,600,000 lbs and the IV second stage 200,000 lbs. Height of the vehicle including the spacecraft was 224 feet. It provided a full scale rehearsal for the coming attempts at a moon landing and a rigorous test of the three modules of the* **Apollo** *craft*

Saturn V

The *Saturn* rockets had no military objectives. They were the first series the Americans had produced as genuine space vehicles. *Saturn I* and *IB* were stages in the development of the giant *Saturn V*.

The three stages of the rocket generate a total of 8,700,000-lb. thrust in 17 minutes of cumulative firing. Stage one is a cluster of five engines, each of 1,500,000-lb. thrust. Firing simultaneously, they lift the 2,750 tons of vehicle 40 miles up and to a speed of over 5,000 m.p.h. in slightly under 2½ minutes.

Eight retro-rockets detach the first stage when it has cut off and the second stage commences firing. The second stage is also a cluster of five engines, but smaller than those in stage one. Stage two burns liquid hydrogen and liquid oxygen and produces a total 1,000,000-lb. thrust over a six-minute burn. Planned performance of this stage is an altitude of 114 miles and a speed of 15,300 m.p.h. The reserve of power built into this design was demonstrated on the *Apollo 13* flight, when the centre engine of the second stage went out halfway through the burn. Despite

The giant **Saturn V**, *above, was produced expressly to get men on the moon before 1970. On take-off it consumes 900 tons of kerosene and liquid oxygen a minute. The huge success of* **Saturn V** *was the turning point in the space race that put America ahead of Russia. From launch pad to the top of the escape tower measures 363 feet and its three stages generate a total of 8,700,000 lbs thrust. In 2½ minutes it is capable of lifting the whole 2,750 tons of vehicle to a height of 40 miles and a speed of over 5,000 m.p.h.*

this loss of thrust, the craft continued its flight into orbit simply by burning a few seconds longer on the third-stage engine. Blow-off of stage two is at just under nine minutes from launching.

The third stage is a *Saturn IVB*, which was the second stage in the *IB* booster. It is a single-chamber engine, also fuelled by hydrogen and oxygen, and generating a thrust of 200,000-lb. Its function is to raise the craft to orbital speed – 17,400 m.p.h. – at a mean altitude of about 120 miles. This takes a burning time of about $2\frac{1}{2}$ minutes and the engine is then shut down while the craft goes into orbit round the earth. Then, when all is ready for the onward journey, the rocket is re-lit and fires for another five minutes or so to raise the speed to earth escape-velocity, which is around 24,400 m.p.h.

Precision as well as power is the important factor in the operation of the third-stage rocket. Too high an escape-velocity would send the payload spinning off into outer space, and, although the crew could overcome this by using their *Service Module's* rocket engines, it would put an end to the lunar objective. Similarly, the right velocity must be reached at the correct moment to fling the craft out of earth orbit in line with the moon rendezvous.

The third stage, jettisoned at about 11,000 miles on moon trajectory, has no fewer than 14 auxiliary control rockets and can still be navigated by ground control. On the *Apollo 13* flight, it was kept more or less in company with the *Apollo* spacecraft and then – for seismic test purposes – was allowed to crash into the moon at a controlled speed. When the *Lunar Module* was sent crashing back to the moon after its crew had re-embarked for the return journey, the moon echoes were so interesting that this further test was planned for the next flight. The *Saturn V* is thus proving a flexible as well as an efficient tool for space exploration.

The Apollo Programme

Apollo, the spacecraft designed for the manned moon flights, consists of several separate parts. The only part of the huge rocket/spacecraft assembly to carry out the entire trip and return to earth is the relatively tiny nosecap called the *Command Module.*

Ahead of it is the escape tower, which is jettisoned during the second stage of the ascent, and behind it is the *Service Module*, which is an engine room for the actual spaceflight. It has drive and control rockets for braking into moon orbit and speeding up again for the return trip. It provides electric power for all the instruments and computer systems, oxygen to breathe and an air-conditioning and temperature control system.

Linking the rocket's three stages with the *Service Module* is the instrument unit, popularly known as the wedding ring. It is a ring-shaped array of guidance and navigational systems, 22 feet in

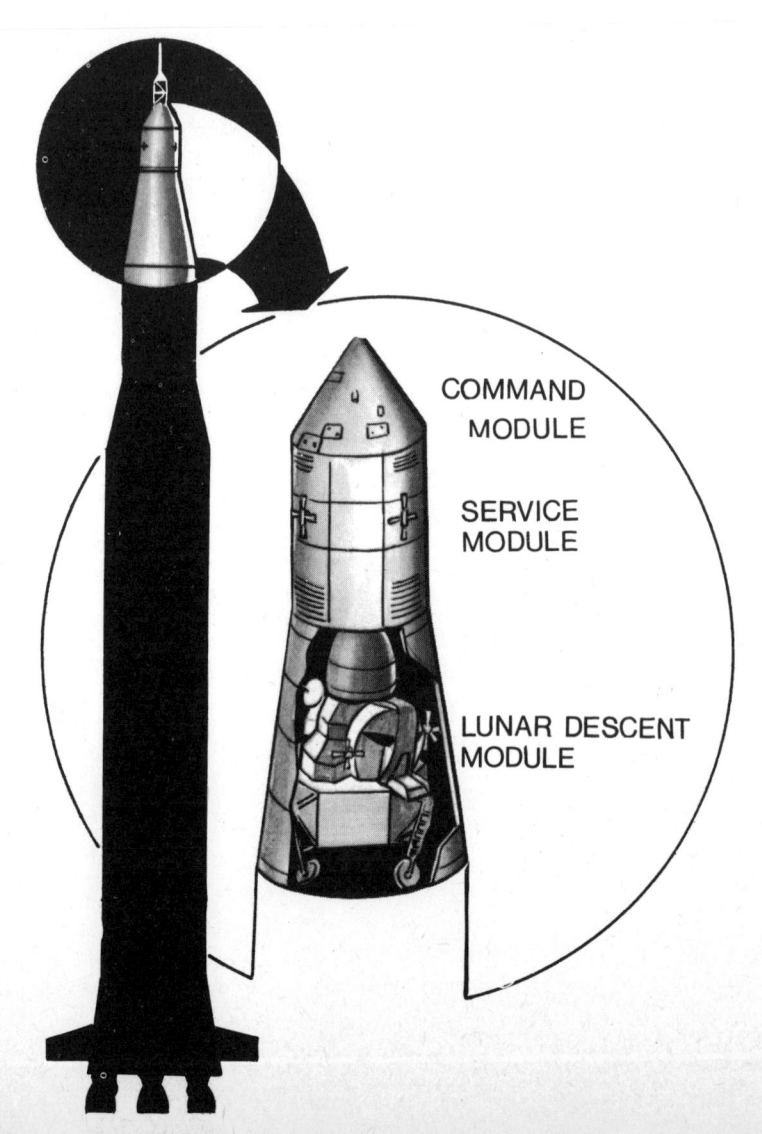

In space the command and service modules detach from the rocket and turn round to dock nose to nose with the lunar module. The lunar module is equipped to land and do a survey of the moon and then bring the astronauts back again to the command ship for return to earth

*Right, the **Apollo** vehicle with capsule atop ready for lift off. Inset is an enlarged detail of the capsule section*

diameter by three feet deep. Its job is to get the spacecraft into the correct place at the scheduled time, travelling in the right direction for moon orbit approach; when it has done all that, it is jettisoned with the third stage of the launch vehicle.

Sitting in an extension of the third-stage rocket is the *Lunar Module* – a delicate and complicated piece of machinery which has to be shielded during take-off.

Until the disaster of January, 1967, when three American astronauts were burned to death in a practice count down, the Americans had always used pure oxygen inside their craft, as was the practice in military aircraft. The Russians used air in their larger craft, but *Apollo's* designers preferred to save weight and space with a one-gas atmosphere.

After that tragedy the craft were modified to take an oxygen/nitrogen mixture during the ascent, changing to low-pressure oxygen when safely out in space. The change-over delayed the programme for nearly two years and it was not until October 11th, 1968, that the first manned *Apollo* flight was made. Walter Schirra, with two previous space flights to his credit, Donn Eisele and Walter Cunningham, spent 11 days in earth orbit and thoroughly tested all the functioning of the *Apollo* spacecraft guidance, control and re-entry systems. As the big rocket was not needed for an earth orbit launch, this flight was carried by a *Saturn IB,* two-stage booster.

Saturn V was used for the first time in a manned launch on December 21st, 1968, when *Apollo 8* took off for an orbit of the moon. The crew were Frank Borman, James Lovell and William Anders, and they spent Christmas making 10 orbits of the moon before returning safely to earth.

There was one more moon flight before an actual attempt at landing was made. James McDivitt, David Scott and Russell Schweikart took off in *Apollo 9* in February, 1969. The moon had been circled, photographed and instrument-landed. The way was now open for the first manned landing.

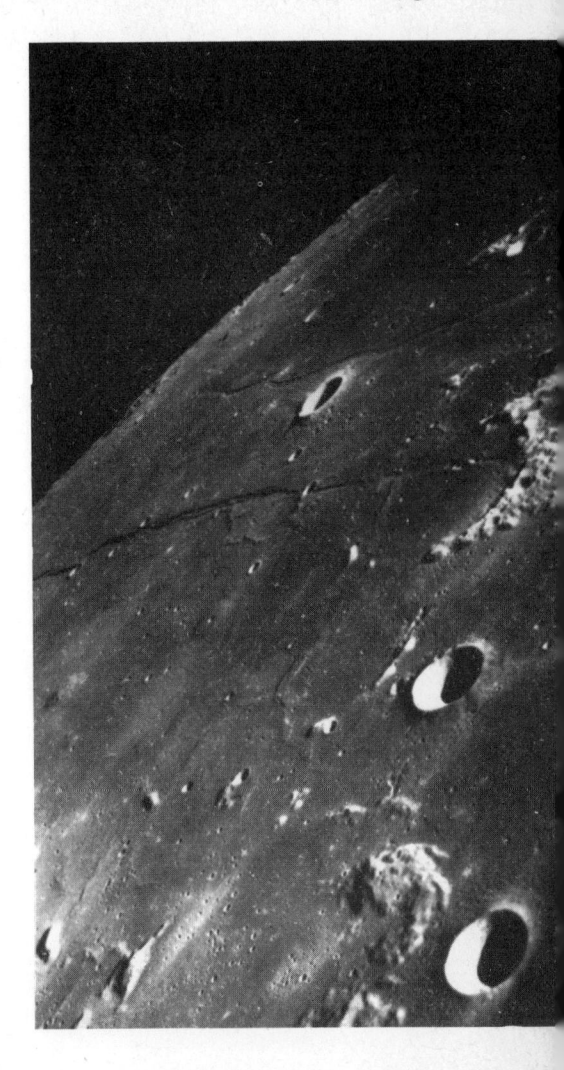

An astronaut's view of the moon's surface

On July 21st, 1969, men walked on the moon. After walking, jumping and collecting samples, they had a telephone conversation from their mooncraft, *Apollo 11,* with the President of the United States, Richard Nixon.

Lunarnauts Neil Armstrong and Edward Aldrin carried out a programme of work, deploying instruments, collecting samples, and experimenting on the limits of their own work capacity and mobility.

Carrying a massive back pack, Aldrin demonstrated in front of the television camera that he could travel in controlled jumps quite quickly. After two and a quarter hours on the surface, the men returned to their spacecraft, loaded up the samples and, six hours later, took off to rejoin Mike Collins in their Command ship, leaving cameras and recording equipment on the moon for the next team to check.

Undoubtedly the most important part of the *Apollo 11* moon flight was the simple fact that it was successful. Now future flights could be planned on the basis of the work they could do on the moon itself.

Apollo 12 took off on November 14th, with Charles Conrad in command, Alan Bean, and Richard

The incredible achievement of putting man on the moon was made possible by the dedication and determination of man and the machines he built for the task. Below is a detailed key diagram of a vital part of that machinery – the **Apollo** *spacecraft command and service modules*

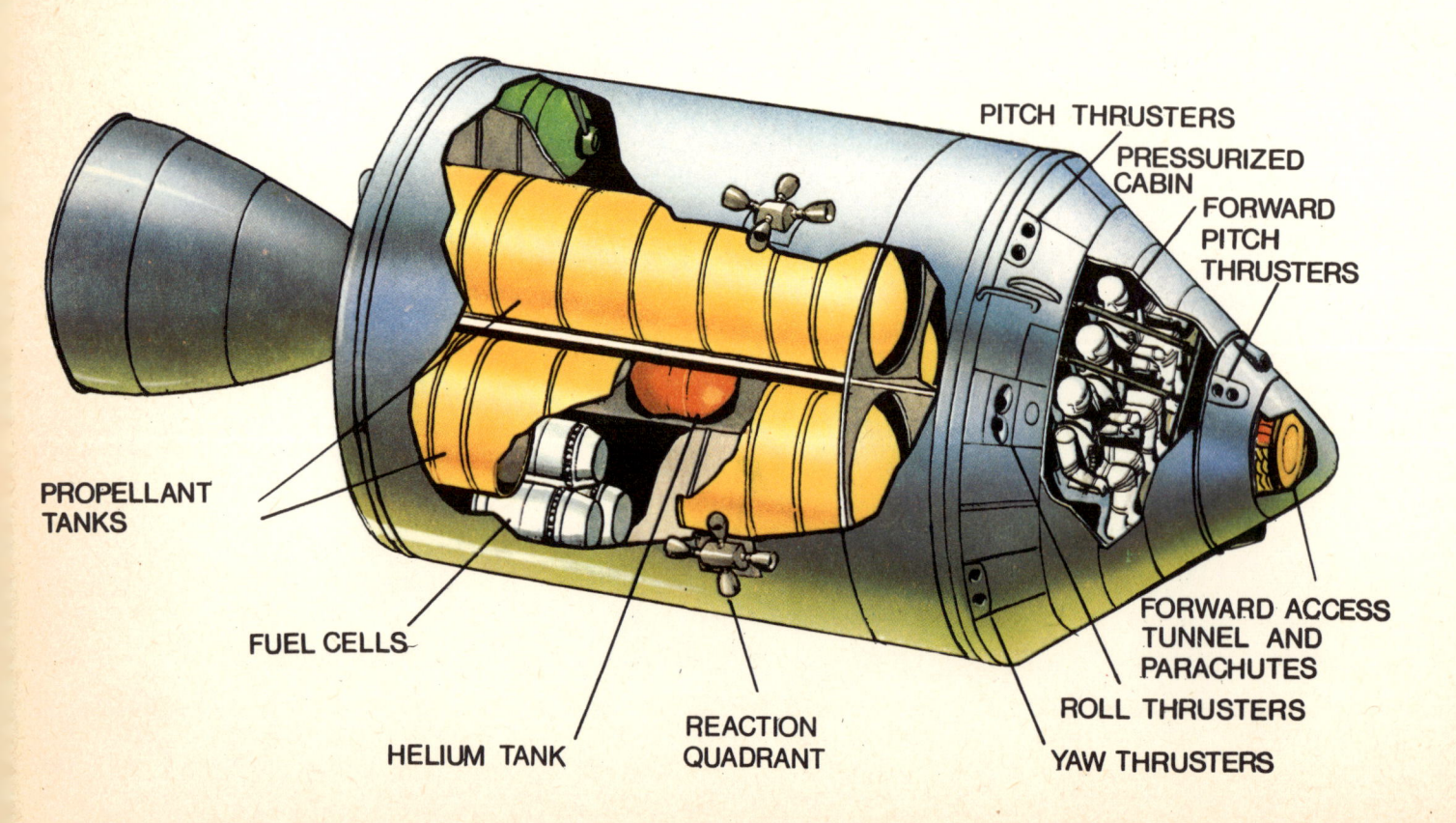

PROPELLANT TANKS
FUEL CELLS
HELIUM TANK
REACTION QUADRANT
PITCH THRUSTERS
PRESSURIZED CABIN
FORWARD PITCH THRUSTERS
FORWARD ACCESS TUNNEL AND PARACHUTES
ROLL THRUSTERS
YAW THRUSTERS

Gordon as pilot. It was part of the mission to recover parts of *Surveyor* to study the effects of moon exposure.

The *Apollo 12* crew found working conditions comparatively easy and reported that future crews should be able to do a full day's work, with only an hour's break for lunch. They left behind them a small nuclear-powered science station designed to collect information about the moon and relay it back to earth.

Although the *Apollo 13* moon landing was abandoned when the *Service Module* blew up on the lunar approach, the mission was by no means a failure. The emergency operation that finally brought astronauts James Lovell, Fred Haise and John Swigert safely back on April 17th, 1970, was a tough test of the capacity and flexibility of the American control systems. The use of the *Lunar Landing Vehicle* as a reserve power unit and life-support system proved the practicability of this form of 'lifeboat' equipment.

The moon is nearly a quarter of a million miles away; it is one fiftieth of the earth's volume but only one hundredth of its mass. It may be hollow, as these figures and the *Apollo* seismic echo tests suggest. But certainly we know more about it now than we did before the *Apollo* flights.

The Russians are now building a space station to enable them to study the moon continuously; the Americans already have their plans laid for future flights. Whatever happens next, Man's conquest of space will go on.

Future means of examining the moon and its make-up include space stations – the Russians are building one now – and **'Molabs'**. *Seen left is a drawing of a mobile laboratory – or 'Molab' – in which long distance moon exploration will one day be carried out. The Russians have already landed a wheeled robot vehicle,* **Limokhod,** *which has carried out short-range exploration*

Launching Sites

In the early days the position of launching sites was determined by the power and range of the rockets to be tested. Semi-desert country was used with aiming ranges of 200 miles and empty space around to accommodate mistakes. The advantage of fully land-based sites is that the test firings can be recovered and studied. As rockets grew bigger, however, sites had to be found that provided for firing over the sea.

The best spot for a space launch is on the equator, where the earth's speed of rotation is 0.46 kilometres a second (over 1,000 m.p.h.). This is helpful in building up to escape velocity.

Furthermore, the earth is itself travelling in its own orbit around the sun at 29.8 km./sec., so that this, in effect, becomes the starting speed for interplanetary voyaging. Mars, which circles the sun in a wider orbit than the earth, has a year of 687 earth days and travels at a speed of 21.5 km./sec. This means that a spacecraft from earth has to speed up after launching to fly out to the Martian orbit. There it will catch up with Mars and then have to slow down to go into orbit around the planet.

Venus reverses this position. It takes a smaller orbit than earth but travels at 35 km./sec. on a 225-day year. A spacecraft to *Venus* has to fly backwards once clear of earth gravity, using its rockets to slow down its sun orbital speed in order to fall inwards towards the sun until it reaches the Venutian orbit. Then it has to speed up to match the speed of the planet.

The next planet to be visited is Jupiter. Unfortunately, it will take nearly three years for a spacecraft to reach Jupiter and, by the time the planet's satellites have been surveyed and the correct 'window' for taking off on the return flight to earth

The earth turns on its axis once a day. The diagram shows that a point on the equator has further to travel to complete one revolution than points at higher latitudes and is therefore moving faster. The best spot for a space launch is evidently on the equator where the speed of rotation is 0.46 kilometres a second – over 1,000 m.p.h. This is an added bonus in build-up to the velocity 'kick' into outer space

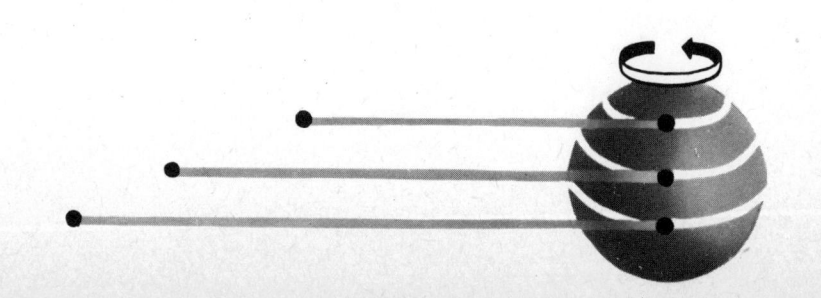

has been awaited, well over six years will have gone by. This is more than we can contemplate in manned flight, so our explorations to Jupiter will be by unmanned probes.

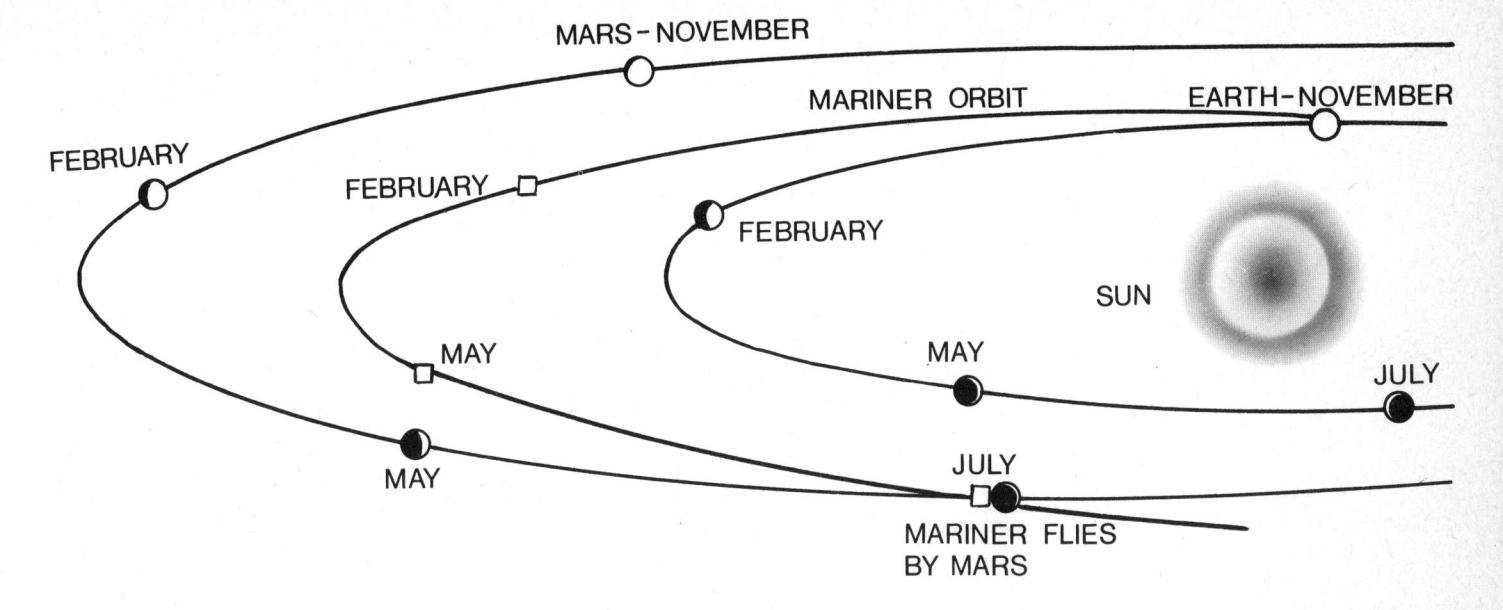

Even for our relatively near neighbour, Mars, the journey with its orbital wait and return will take fifteen months, and we cannot visualise a spaceship large enough to support a number of humans for that length of time. It is true that there are shorter routes than the tangential linking of orbits, but these would require enormous power outputs – smaller craft and bigger rockets.

This kind of exploration is really the job of the space observatory – hardly as romantic a notion as spacemen, but much more useful.

To fly out to a Martian orbit a spacecraft from earth would have to speed up after launching, for Mars circles the sun in a wider orbit than earth. Above is **Mariner 4** *describing a typical Mars trajectory*

As Venus makes a smaller orbit of the sun than earth does, a spacecraft from earth would need to fly backwards once clear of the earth's gravity. Below **Mariner 2** *describes a typical trajectory*

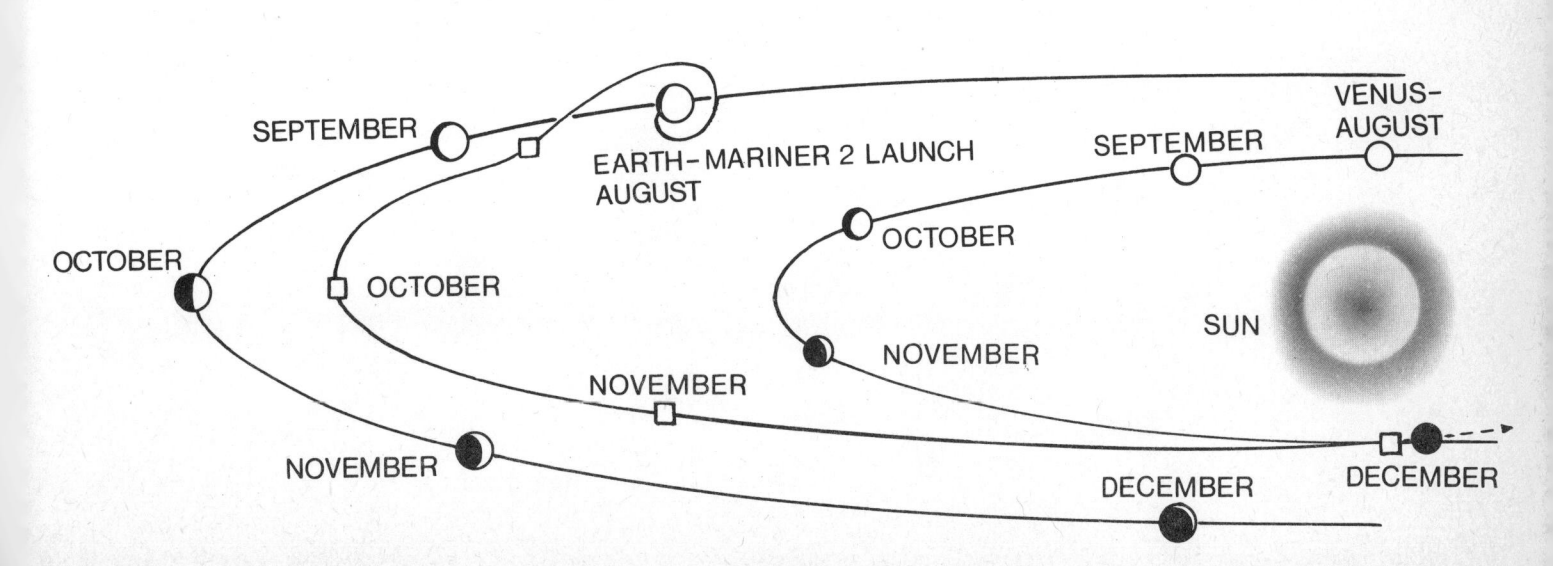

The Back-Up

Space vehicles, whether manned or unmanned, need enormous back-up forces to get them off the ground and monitor their activities in flight. The men who do the actual launching work within a few yards of the launching pad itself. They operate from a block-house – a low concrete building with walls several feet thick and steel shutters over windows and doors.

There are usually about 35 men involved in the final firing schedule, which may take 12 hours. This is the time taken to check and re-check the electrical equipment that will control the stages of preparation. Inside the blockhouse is a panel with lights for each phase of the procedure. Each light must come on as each move is initiated and a red cut-off light indicates when the operation is completed.

The whole programme is rehearsed again and again, so that all the circuits are proven and all the operators know exactly what they have to do and thereby time their movements to the second.

While this is going on inside the blockhouse, the men on the rocket and gantry are making their own physical checks and sealing the access doors. This completed, the crew fit the nose blow-off explosives. Then fuelling starts.

Each constituent is loaded separately and in specific order: first alcohol, then peroxide, then liquid oxygen. If there is any trouble – as, for example, when the oxygen freezes the fuel traps – a crewman must go up and deal with it while the count-down is held at that point until the trouble is remedied. Meanwhile, the launch pad is gradually cleared of personnel and equipment. The gantry is moved away, the trucks, trailers and fire pumps withdrawn and finally only the rocket itself remains on the pad as the safety man turns his key and moves back into the blockhouse.

Fuelling is always a tense procedure and things can go wrong at this stage. The fuels are dangerous to handle, and a splash can mean a serious burn;

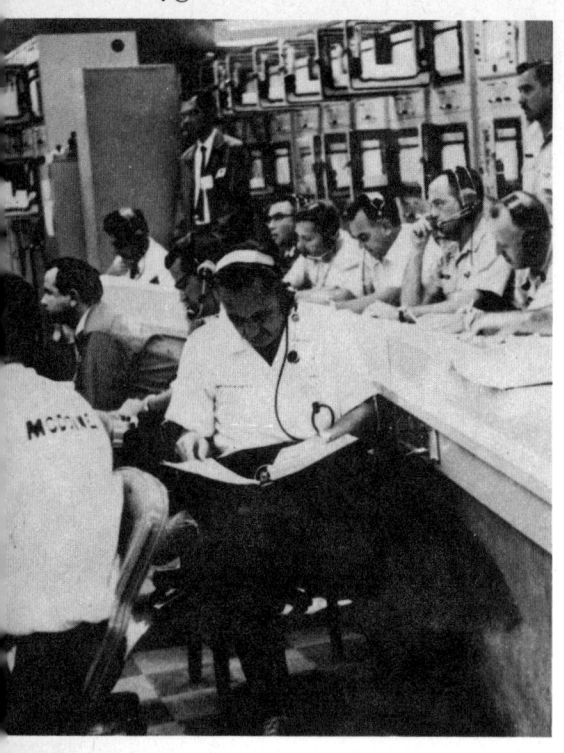

Rocketry scientists and service personnel in the blockhouse rehearsing a countdown. Approximately 35 men are involved in the final firing schedule which may take 12 or more hours before the actual launch

metals become brittle and contract in contact with the liquid oxygen; controls which move easily on test become stiff or jam during the fuelling process. Any of these snags can cause a hold-up in the countdown procedure.

When the key is brought in there are still about 15 minutes to go before the firing button is pressed. The gas pressure is brought up to level, the electrical power inside the rocket is switched on, circuit by circuit, then the hydraulic power comes in.

As each section inside the blockhouse completes its task, the red light on the appropriate panel goes out and the green comes on. Not until the whole panel shows green can the count reach the stage where the fuel tanks are pressurised, the recorders switched on and the final seconds counted aloud. When the button is pressed for firing, the blockhouse men have done their job. Now the tracking and control stations will assume control, and hundreds of men spread over thousands of miles will take over the guidance and control of the flight.

The **Saturn Apollo** *Launch Complex at* **Cape Kennedy**

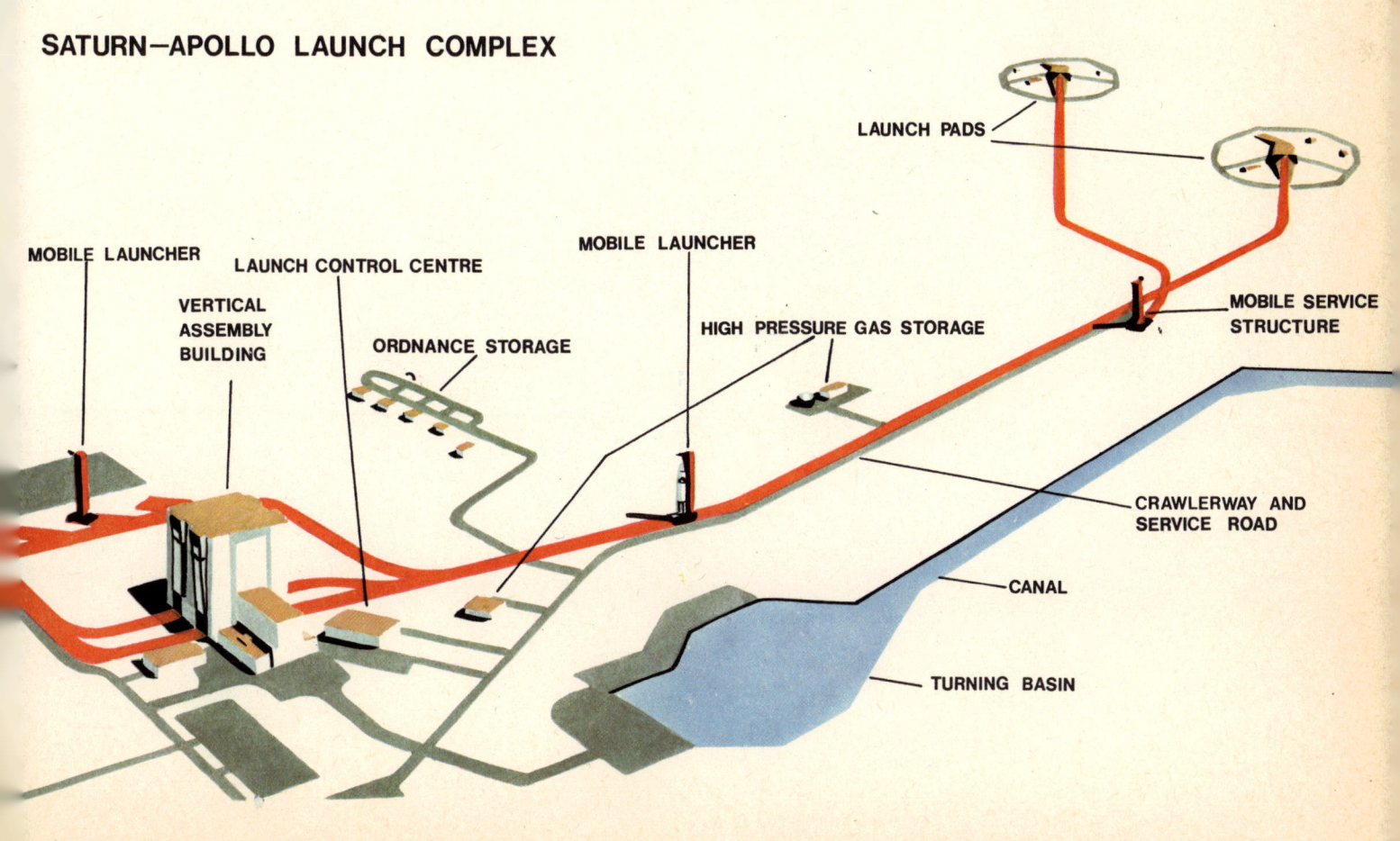

SATURN—APOLLO LAUNCH COMPLEX

Nuclear Rockets

If we are to send up bigger spaceships over longer distances we need more efficient engines, and it is natural in the atomic age to look to the nuclear heat motor to provide the next stage in space transport.

Work on these lines began to be taken seriously when the Americans made a successful static test run of the *Kiwi–A* in July, 1959. Power output was understood to be unimpressive and elaborate precautions were taken against radio-active contamination, including firing the rocket from a railcar two miles from the control centre, then waiting nearly a week for the radio-activity to fall off before examining the results. The system was found to work.

The principle of the nuclear rocket is that a reactor provides the controlled heat which vaporises a liquid fuel. The resultant expansion of the fuel – usually liquid hydrogen – provides the thrust. The latest developed nuclear rocket engines were returning specific impulse figures of 800 to 1000 seconds (i.e., the theoretical time over which a pound of fuel will produce a pound of thrust) when budget cuts stopped the project in 1969.

After several *Kiwi–A* tests had proved successful, tenders were sought at the end of 1960 for more advanced reactors, and testing of the *Kiwi–B* series started in November, 1962. Some teething troubles were experienced and various experimental units

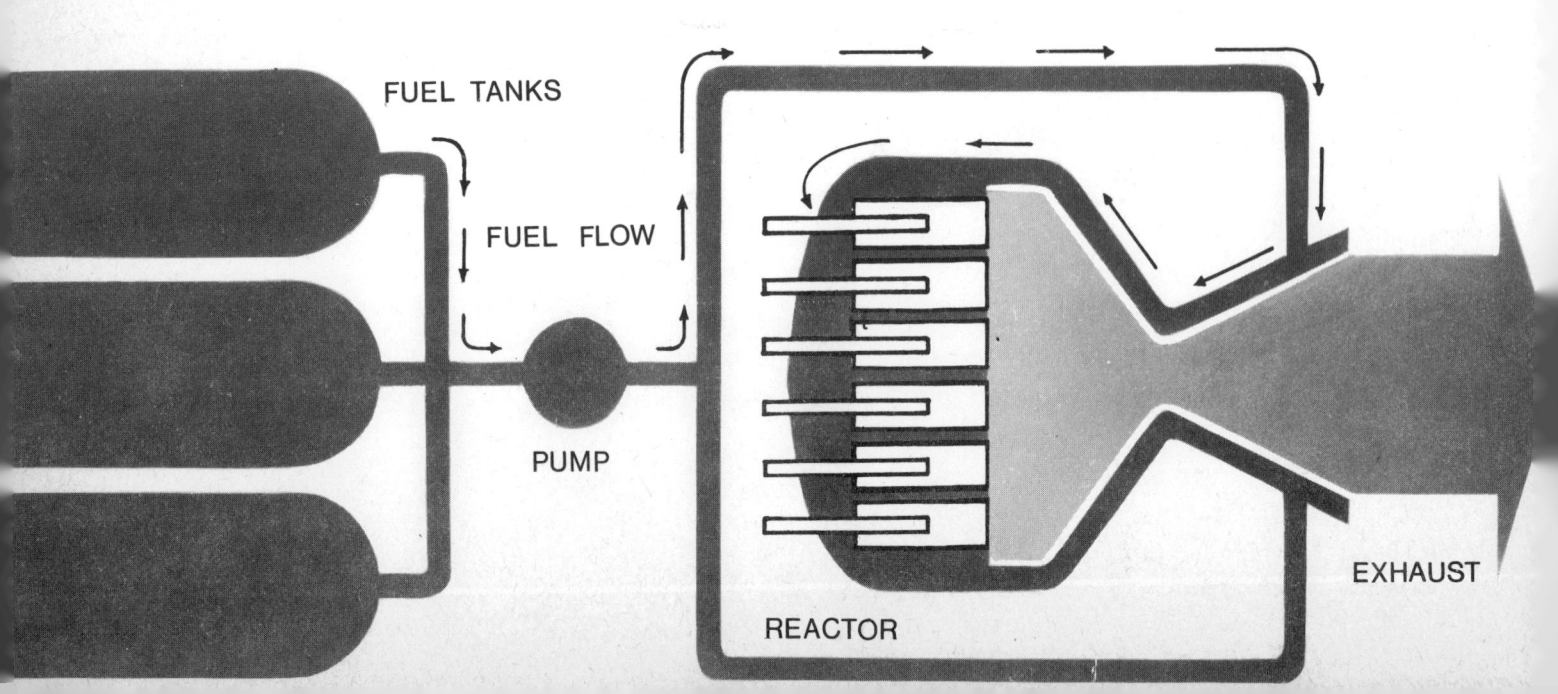

*With space engineers' concern for fuel efficiency it is natural that the next stage in space transport should be focussed on the nuclear heat motor. First tests along these lines were made by the Americans as long ago as 1959 with a successful static test run of the **Kiwi-A**. The last model tested in the series was the **Kiwi B4E** (shown above) which showed in a August/September 1964 that that it could also be shut off for long periods and restarted when required*

Shown below is the layout of a simple nuclear power plant

tried out. In all, eight of these reactors were built and tested successfully.

At the last testing on August 28th, 1964, *Kiwi B4E* was shut down after a satisfactory performance and left standing. It was restarted on September 10th to prove that it could be cut off for long periods on space flight and restarted for the return journey.

The basic problems having been solved by the *Kiwi* programme, the next phase was NERVA (Nuclear Engine For Rocket Vehicle Application). A vehicle was on the drawing board under the name of RIFT (Reactor In Flight Test) which it was intended to launch into space by a *Saturn V* rocket for test in 1967. However, the project was cancelled before the vehicle was built and it is now unlikely the NERVA will ever fly.

In order to continue the experiments with small reactors, the *Phoebus* programme was instituted. The objective was to get longer sustained power from reactors of the size and type of *Kiwi,* and to keep the research lines of NERVA open. What has already been achieved is a significant space step towards nuclear-powered flight. The last of the NERVA tests produced a thrust of 250,000-lb. The engine could be stopped and restarted at will and – a worthwhile design point – the restart technique required no outside source of ignition. Reactor heat and hydrogen pressure alone were sufficient, even under low temperature conditions.

The *Phoebus* programme of tests continues and the second series of motors is now undergoing evaluation.

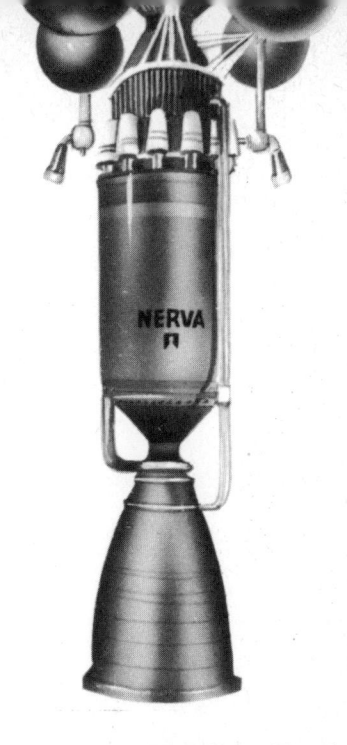

The **Nerva** *(Nuclear Engine For Rocket Vehicle Application) was originally intended to be launched into space by a* **Saturn V** *rocket in 1967. This programme was subsequently cancelled but not before some very successful tests had been made. Now it seems that* **Nerva** *will never fly. The last* **Nerva** *test produced a thrust of 250,000 lbs. Experimental programmes with small reactors are continuing today using the valuable experience gained by such series as* **Nerva**

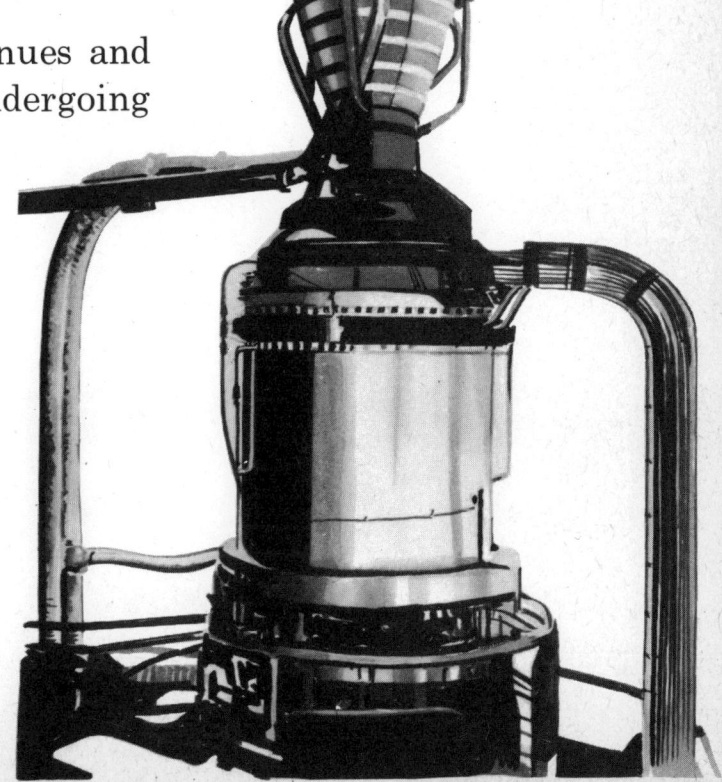

Cancelled

The enormous number of projects involving rocketry that have been started since World War II range from tactical missiles for battlefields to interplanetary travel. Inevitably, many of them never get past the stage of drawings or mock-ups. Some get to the experimental stage before being dropped. Some are even developed and then cancelled.

There are all sorts of reasons for these decisions. It may be an economy drive at government level that cuts back the research work, or it may be that the experiments are not promising enough. In such a fast-moving field, a cancellation may be due to the fact that the project was outdated by other developments.

Not all the work done is lost by a cancellation. Lessons learned on one project can be utilised on another. *Navaho,* for example, never flew operationally, but it provided the basis of the *Atlas* rocket. In some cases, the programmes are not so much cancelled as put in cold storage.

One of these was *Project Dyna-Soar,* the wingless plane. It was cancelled while still in the glider phase of its testing and never flew under rocket power. But because there is such a great need for this type of craft as a ferry or rescue plane, there is no doubt that all the work done on *Dyna-Soar* will be used on a similar project fairly soon.

Likewise, the atomic engines – *Kiwi* and *Nerva* – never took to the air. But research is still going on in the modified programme *Phoebus,* and a small self-drive, reactor-engined final-stage craft can be built, as and when required, on the basis of the work already done.

Navaho was, in a way, the starting point of the change-over from purely military to space research development. A rocket-launched but ramjet-powered pilotless plane, *Navaho,* was so new a concept that it was difficult to decide on a name for it. It started off as *MX–770,* changed to bomber classification *XB–64,*

*The **Navaho**. A rocket launched ramjet-powered pilotless plane which was fired vertically. It carried its payload not on its nose but on its back. The payload was a stubby-winged supersonic plane*

then became a missile, *XSM–64,* and finally just *Project Navaho.*

The rocket was a three-engined, liquid-fuelled unit, 70 feet long, which fired vertically for take-off but carried its payload on its back rather than in its nose. The payload was a stubby-winged supersonic plane (Mach 2·2 was actually achieved in level flight) powered by an experimental variety of engines, the final choice being a *Curtiss-Wright RJ47* of 40,000-lb. thrust. Its flight plan was to climb vertically on the first-stage booster to 100,000 feet, drive 30,000 feet to gain speed, then level out and go for its target.

With hindsight, it does not seem surprising that the development of the *Atlas* rocket and the *Snark* guided missile offered a cheaper and simpler solution to the problem, and the *Navaho* project was eventually cancelled in 1967. But before it died, *Navaho* carried instruments to great heights to study high-altitude turbulence effects; it had also been the centre of development for new metallurgical techniques that have been used in later and lighter spacecraft.

Another cancelled programme was *Project Nova* – the plan for the super rocket vehicle. It had been planned to build clusters of huge rockets, and the possibility was envisaged of no fewer than 20 engines in a giant assembly 500 feet long and 70 feet in diameter, producing a thrust of 6,000,000-lb. It was to be liquid-fuelled on hydrogen and oxygen.

The project was beaten by fuelling problems. The best pumps available put in 2,500 gallons a minute, but they could not pump in the fuel faster than it evaporated. It was estimated that a one-hour hold-up in the count-down could cost £500,000 in lost fuel alone. And so *Nova* was cancelled in 1961.

Project Nova . . . *a super rocket vehicle 500 feet long powered by 20 engines. It was conceived at a time when the Americans were badly shaken by the size and power of the huge Russian rockets, but it was never built*

The Rocket Industry

The question of whether we can afford space programmes at all is often discussed both at social and political levels. There are many who firmly believe that the vast amounts of money and specialised scientific resources employed could be put to better use for the added comfort of mankind on earth. The discussions are generally futile, because the space race is as inevitable in its way as was the invention of the wheel, the steam engine or the electric light bulb. Man must search for knowledge or civilisation will collapse.

Nevertheless, it is as well to examine the balance sheet of space flight to date and see what the facts reveal. What has gone into modern rocketry, instrumentation, telemetry and astral navigational equipment has been a diversion of scientific effort and technical and financial resources rather than an extra expenditure in any of those fields. If there

Centaur second stage engines on the assembly line (below)

Assembling a communications satellite (right)

had been no rocket weapons produced and left over from World War II, there would have been something else of equal cost and complexity. Supersonic pilotless aircraft, for example, could have had the same appeal if they had been found practicable before the ballistic missile was created.

These would certainly have cost more than rockets and would probably have been of less use to mankind. The rocket motor works efficiently in airless space and is the only kind of drive yet discovered that does. Because it has been brought to near perfection in the space race, we can see live television pictures of events round the world by satellite relay, we can forecast the paths of hurricanes and effectively police military adventurism by the major powers of the world.

The car required better springs than the horse cart – and got them; the aeroplane needed lighter and stronger metals than the car; the space rocket requires more powerful propellent fuels than the jet plane; and so the process of development and improvement of techniques and the production of new materials goes on into the space age.

Satellites observing and photographing the earth are already of practical use in areas ranging from forest fire detection to geological surveying. Even the extent of crop disease has been established by satellite survey. As the satellites grow into manned space laboratories, so will the knowledge gained perfect new techniques. It has already been forecast that space factories operating in zero gravity conditions will be able to make a range of high-quality goods from optical lenses to ball bearings to higher standards of accuracy than is possible on earth. The whole of industry thus benefits from some of the fall-out of space research.

It is regrettable, but nevertheless true, that wars have always speeded up the invention and development of technical novelties. Space rockets came out of war, but now the use of them provides the same stimulus without the need for further wars. For this let us be truly grateful.

New techniques for handling the gigantic and the minute. Technicians prepare a huge handling fixture for the Saturn booster.

Vacuum cleaning under a microscope for clinical cleanliness of components

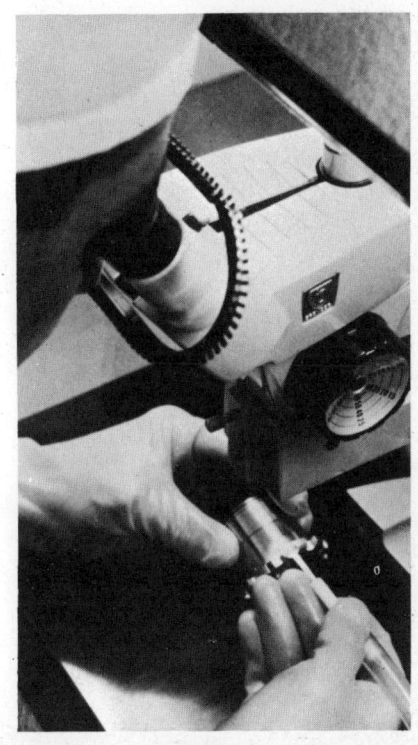

Odd-Ideas

As so many of the things now happening in space travel research would have seemed like the dreams of madmen a few years ago, one hesitates to condemn any idea, however far-fetched. But there are some suggestions made on the slimmest of evidence that are obviously non-starters.

One scheme is the equivalent of a sun-powered steamship, using the sun to power space flight. Usually called the solar boiler, this has a practical basis in that the heat from the sun would be greater as one travels towards the source. A journey to Venus, for example, would expose the ship to double the heat intensity experienced on earth.

As solar energy is already used to charge the batteries of satellites and heat houses in California, there is some reason for thinking that it could also drive spaceships. Unfortunately, the only way to use the heat would be to boil a fluid (it could be water, but the most efficient medium would be hydrogen) and use the resultant high-pressure gas to drive the ship.

The question of using atomic power in space has long occupied the minds of space scientists. The huge power of an atomic explosion would render obsolete the early space calculation of 1,000 lbs of rocket to put one lb of payload into space. With atomic forces at their command scientists could think more in terms of lb for lb. Seen here is one of the many ideas dreamed up in this context. It is the 'Schmoo' – named after a popular American comic strip character – which was envisaged as being propelled by small atomic explosions

However good the theory, in practice this would have no advantage over current liquid-fuelled rockets. The ship would still have to be supplied with the propellent fluid for the sun to heat, and the solar ray collecting-dish would have to be movable in all directions to face the sun, whatever the direction of the ship. The weight and complication of this system would be far greater than straight rocketry.

Some odd ideas come from most unexpected places. It was from the Lockheed Space Division that the idea came of using an atomic pile to power a thermo-electric generator. The power would be used to vaporise a fuel in the craft to create an ion drive.

Because the pile would be so highly radioactive that nothing could live near it, it was proposed that the pile should be towed by the spaceship on a cable a mile long. All the arithmetic worked out well and the power/weight ratios were attractive. But how the thing was to be launched or landed, and what would happen if the trailer jack-knifed, were never figured out.

The huge forces released by a few pounds of fissile material in atomic bombs have naturally led many inventive minds to think in terms of atomic explosion drives. Figures given for such bombs usually refer to their power in terms of thousands of tons of TNT, and it seems obvious that the old rule-of-thumb calculation of the early space rocket pioneers of 1000-lb. of rocket to put one lb. of payload into space could be neatly changed to a pound for a pound formula by the use of atomic power.

Plans for controlled explosions – lots of small bangs instead of one big one – have been advanced time after time, but the laws of physics are against them and bomb drive is unlikely to figure in the realities of space flight.

A solar sail. The discovery of the solar wind revived an early idea of huge ships that literally sailed in space. The wind – particles of light rays from the sun – is of such low intensity that it would take a sail of 4 million square feet to collect one lb of pressure. On this basis the idea of the wind used as a propellant must surely remain in the realms of fiction

Electric Systems

Very little power is required to accelerate and control an object of any size in the free-fall conditions of space. Hence the attractions of the idea of photon, or – more correctly – ion drive, for really long-range space flights.

Once a spacecraft is in orbit round the earth after being launched by conventional rockets, the steady application of any pressure, however tiny, would keep it accelerating until sooner or later escape velocity was reached and the ship went out into space. If the same pressure were maintained, the acceleration would continue until the craft attained the speed of light. After that, no one knows what would happen.

For manned flights, the idea of taking a few weeks to get out of orbit and a few months to pick up a useful cruising speed in space is not worth study. The maintenance of life-support systems for these extra days, weeks or months would cost more in take-off load than any possible advantage the drive system could provide. But for unmanned probes, the time factors are of less importance. A probe that circled the earth for a week or so could be usefully employed during that time in sending back a stream of valuable information. So ion drive is a likely prospect in space exploration proper, but not for the transportation of humans in space.

The principle of the ion drive rocket is that some basic alkali metal fuel – like sodium, potassium or caesium – is vaporised, then ionized, and the ions accelerated by an electric or magnetic field. The charged ions can be separated into positive and negative streams and sent flying out of the ship's tail through separate thrust nozzles. Outside they meet up, neutralise each other, and enable the ship to travel a little faster each second.

The trouble is, however, that the electric power required is quite considerable and conventional

Photon, or **Ion**, *drive is a likely prospect in the calculations for future space exploration but much more for the unmanned, data collecting flights.* **Ion** *drive vaporises basic alkali metal fuels and accelerates ions by electric power, after ionization. Above is a prototype* **Ion** *engine*

A proposal to send ion rockets into orbit mounted on an **Agena** *vehicle for testing purposes*

generators are hopelessly heavy and bulky for space flight needs.

Nuclear power may yet provide the answer if, and when, some system of conversion to electricity directly from the heat source can be found. Man is on the verge of great discoveries in the realms of physics and it may well be that most of those who read this book will live to comprehend the mysteries of magneto-hydrodynamics and even travel on plasma-wave drives.

One of the facts of nature that has so far defeated all our researches is the phenomenon of gravity. The force that draws particles of matter towards each other, regardless of their chemical composition, and literally holds the world together is still an unknown quantity. No line of enquiry has gone one inch towards understanding it, let alone handling it.

If ever the secret is uncovered and an anti-gravity-charged ship becomes a reality, the whole concept of space flight will be altered. Such a ship could be driven by the power of a beam of light, and steered and stabilised by tiny jets of bottled gas. No one dare say it is impossible, but we can probably all agree that it is somewhat unlikely.

Should an Ion drive spaceship ever become a practical proposition for interplanetary voyages it might look something like this artist's impression. However, present day conventional generators designed to produce the electric power required are so bulky that it may never be feasible

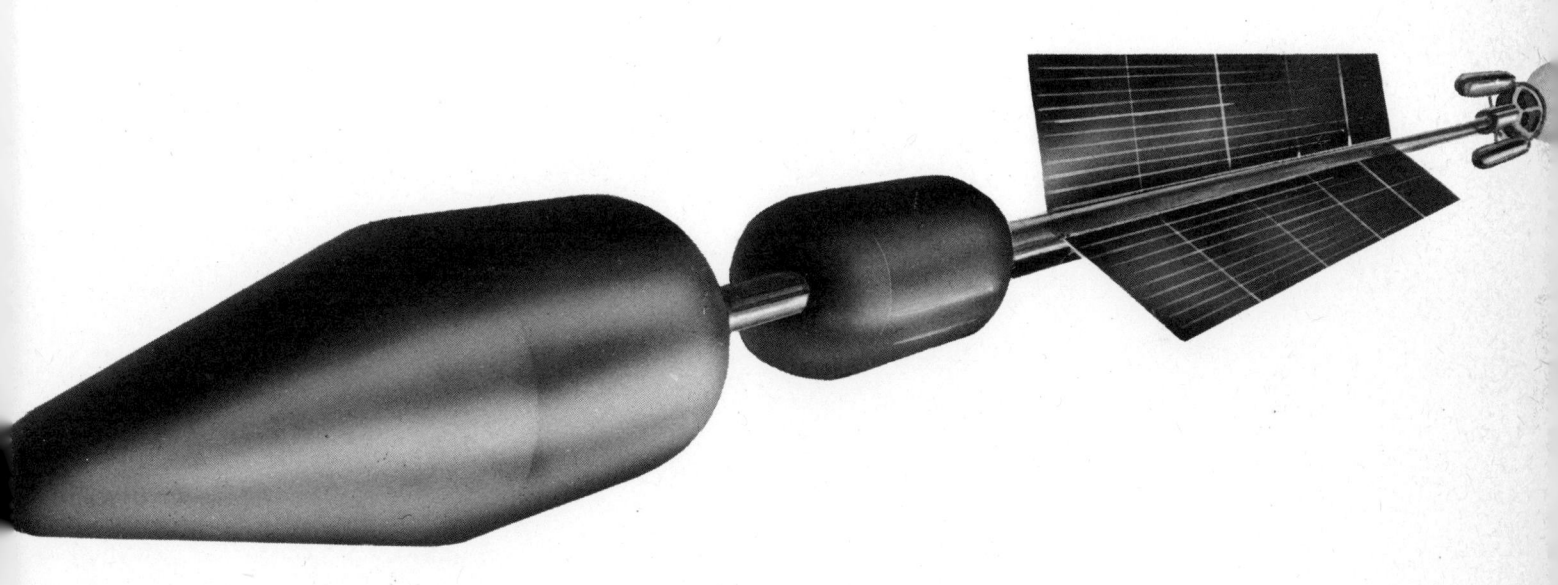

On to the Stars

It is difficult to visualise, even with the aid of a strong imagination, the enormous variations in size, physical content and distance from each other of the planetary and starry bodies.

Men have already walked on the moon and sent controlled probes to Mars and Venus, but these are next-door neighbours of the earth and the distances are microscopic compared with those to the nearest stars in our galaxy. Our sun would only be a speck in the sky if viewed from any other solar system in the galaxy, but this is not all. The galaxy itself is but a relatively small part of a whole universe of galaxies. The fact is that astronomical distances are beyond the practical comprehension of the human mind.

To send a radio message to the nearest star and get an answer back would take about nine years. What then is the point and limit of man's conquest of space?

What our astronauts on the moon and the unmanned probes into space are seeking is new knowledge that could lead to a fresh understanding of the universe we live in. There are side-effects and fringe benefits, of course; new discoveries in electronics and metallurgy, made directly as a result of participation in the space race, will benefit many of us who will never leave the earth. But the drive that kept human civilisation expanding and developing in past ages must go into space if the whole race is not to die of sheer inertia.

Perhaps that is the real significance of space travel. Having learned the limits of the earth and satisfied our material needs from its resources, we must continue the quest for knowledge into fields that have no limits, so that humanity may continue to develop. There are worse objectives than that to work for.

Perhaps it is true, as Einstein suggested, that time stands still at the speed of light. The crew of a

From outer space our galaxy would look like this. The arrow points to the position of our sun. Our galaxy is but a small part of the whole universe of galaxies. Astronomical distances are beyond the practical comprehension of the human mind

spacecraft that could travel at 670,000,000 m.p.h. might spend four million years travelling to the nearest galaxy to our own and return to earth only a little older.

There would probably be no point in their coming back at all, but the idea of the time factor in human life might be the key to ultimate immortality. Whatever fantasies we may dream up for the future of mankind, one thing is certain: there must be fresh targets, ever new objectives for man to work for, or there will be no future at all.

The earth is about 93 million miles from the sun, which lies at the centre of the solar system. Altogether, from one extreme of Pluto's orbit to the other, the solar system is some 3,700 million miles across. This seems huge, but it is insignificant when compared with the distance of 25 million million miles to even the nearest star, Alpha Centauri

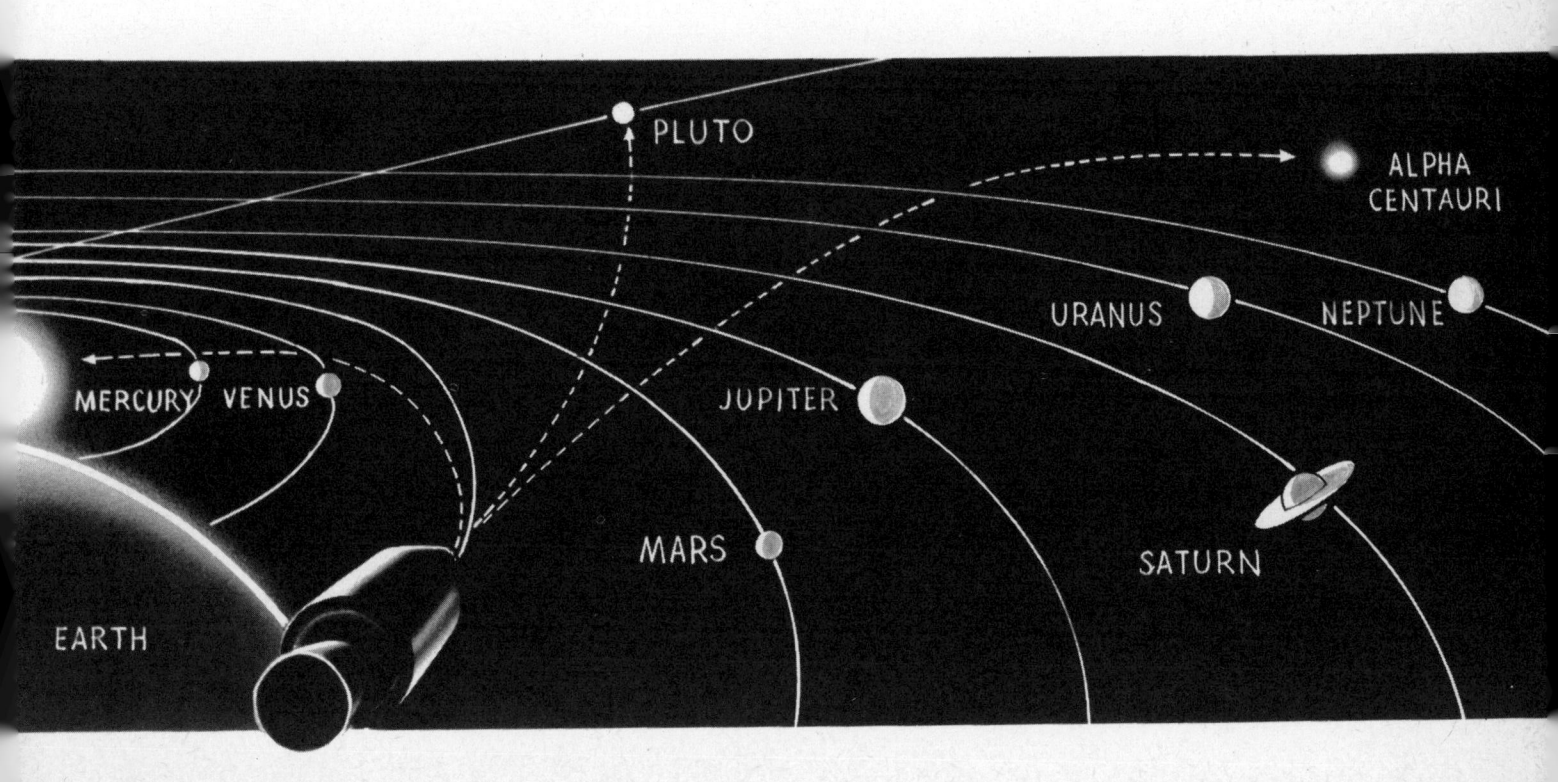

Index

Able rocket, 39, 66
Aerobee weather-probe, 35
Air Force, U.S. (U.S.A.F.), 39, 40, 41, *42, 43, 44*
Aldrin, Edward, 63, 74
Alpha Centauri, *91*
America, *10*, 32, 33, 34, *38-9*, 45, 49, 59, 63, 65, 70, 74
Anders, William, 73
Animals, in space, 74, 51, 58, 60
Anson, frigate, 16
Apollo spacecraft, 36, 68, 69, 71, 72, 73, 74, 75, *79*
Arabia, 13
Ariel satellite, 57
Armstrong, Neil, 63, 74
Army, U.S., 32, 36
Astronauts, 37, 47, *49,* 57, 59, 63, 73, 75
Astronaut's Bay, 67
Atlantic Ocean, 37
Atlas rocket, 25, 26, 37, 39, 48, 55, 56, 57, 59, 63, 68, 82, 83, 84, 86
B-29, 43

Balloons, *see also* Zeppelins
  Montgolfier, 32, 34
  Skyhook, 32
  Sondes (unmanned), 35
Bean, Alan, 74
Bell Aircraft, *40,* 41
Belyayev, Col. Pavel, 61
Boulougne, 14
Borman, Frank, 62, 73
Boxer, Col., 17
Bykovsky, Valery, 61
Byzantium, 13

California, 88
Canopus, 25, 55
Cape Canaveral, *see* Cape Kennedy
Cape Kennedy, 39, 58, 69, *79*
Carpenter, Commander Scott, 59
Centaur engine, 84
Cernan, Eugene, 63
Christmas, 73
Collins, Michael, 63, 74
Congreve, William, 14, 15, 16
Conrad, Charles, 62, 63, 74
Convair, 39
Cooper, Major Gordon, 59, 62
Copenhagen, 14
Cosmonauts, 45, 46
Cunningham, Walter, 73
Curtiss-Wright RJ47, 83

Delta form, 42, 44, 45
  rocket, 56, 57
Diapason satellite, *51*

Distant Space Communications Centre, 64
Dyna-Soar, Project, 44, 82

Earth, 19, *25,* 28, 29, 33, 34, 39, 45, 47, 48, 49, 51, 52, 59, 62, 63, 64, 65, 66, 67, 70, 71, 72, 73, 76, 77, 84, 86, 90, *91*
Edison, 67
Einstein, Albert, 90
Eisele, Donn, 73
Explorer satellite, *50,* 51, 56

Feoktistov, Konstantin, 61
Friendship 7 (Mercury spacecraft), 59
Freedom 7 (Mercury spacecraft), *37,* 58

Gagarin, Major Yuri, 46, 58, 60, 61
Gemini spacecraft, 48, 57, 59, 62, 63
General Electric, 39
Germany, 44
Glenn, Lt.-Col. John, 38, 59
Goddard, Robert H., 20, 21, 30
Gordon, Richard, 63, 74
Greece, 13
Grisson, Capt. Virgil, 58, 62

Haise, Fred, 75
Hale, William, 16

India, 13, 15
Intercontinental Ballistic Missile (I.C.B.M.), 38
International Geophysical Year (1957), 35

Joliot-Curie, *67*
Jupiter, planet, 76, 77, *91*
  rocket, 37, 51

Kiwi (nuclear rocket engine), 80, 81, 82
Komarov, Vladimir, 48, 61
Komet (Messerschmitt), 40

Leonov, Lt.-Col. Aleksei, 61, 62
Little Joe rocket, 36, 37
Lockheed Space Division, 89
London, 32
Lorin, René, 40
Lovell, James, 62, 63, 73, 75
Lovell, Sir Bernard, 10
Luna spacecraft, 66, 67

McDivitt, James, 62, 73
Mare Australe, *67*
  Crisium, *67*
  Foecunditatus, *67*
  Humboldt, *67*

Marginis, *67*
Moscow, *67*
Myechto, *67*
Smythii, *67*
Undarum, *67*
Marine Corps, U.S., 59
Mariner space-probe, 25, 52, 54 55, 77
Mars, *25,* 49, 52, 53, 54, 55, 76, 77, 90, *91*
Martians, 53
Martin, Glenn, 35
Maxwell Lomonosov, *67*
Mercury capsule, 25, 47, 58, 59, 60, 62
  planet, *91*
Midas (anti-I.C.B.M.), 39
Modules, command, 68, 69, 71, 72
  Lunar Excursion, 68, 69, 71, 72 73
  Service, 68, 69, 72, 75
Molab, 74
Mongols, 12
Moon, 20, 46, 48, 49, 52, 59, 66, 67, 68, 69, 71, 72, 73, 74, 75, 90
Mount Palomar (California, U.S.), 65
Muroc Dry Lake, 41
MX-770, 82

Napoleon, 14
National Aeronautics and Space Administration (N.A.S.A.), 39, *45, 47,* 58
Navaho, Project, 82, 83
Naval Research Laboratory, 35
Navy, U.S., 34, 41
Neptune, *91*
Nerva, 81, 82
Newton, Sir Isaac, 15, 26
Nieuport Scout, 16
Nike Cajun, rocket, 35
Nikolayev, 61
Nixon, Richard M., 74
Northdrop HL-10, glider, 45
  M2-F2, 45
Nova rocket, 68, 83

Oberth, Hermann, 20, 21
Opel, Fritz von, 18, 40
Opel Rak I & II, 18

Paris, 35
Peenemunde, 50
Pegasus space-probe, 53
Pershing rocket, 37
Phoebus programme, 81
Pioneer moon probe, 66, 67
Pluto, *91*
Popovich, 61

Ranger moon probe, 56, 67
Reactions Motors Inc., 35

Redstone Arsenal, 32
rocket, 36, 37, 51, 58, 59
RIFT, 81
Royal Arsenal, 14
Russia, *see* U.S.S.R.

Samos satellite, 39
Saturn rocket, 21, 23, 27, 36, 37 68, 69, 70, 71, 73, *79, 81,* 85
Schirra, Commander Walter, 38, 59, 62, 73
Schmoo, 88
Schweikart, Russell, 73
Scott, David, 63, 73
Scout rocket, 36, 37
Seagrave, Henry, 18
Sheperd, Commander Alan, 37, 58
Skynet satellite, 52
Skyrocket (supersonic), 41
Snark missile, 83
Society for Space Travel, 18, 21
Solar System, 25, 49, 52
Soviet Mountains, *67*
Soyuz spacecraft, 48
Sputnik spacecraft, 11, 35, 50, 51, 60, 66
Stafford, Thomas, 62

Sun, 25, 55, 76, *77,* 89, 91
Surveyor spacecraft, 38, 66, 75
Swigert, John, 75

Tereshkova, Valentina, 47, 60, 61
Thor rocket, 38, 66
   see also *Able* rocket
Tiros weather satellite, *51*
Titan missile, 22, 27, 37, 56, 57
   rocket, 44, 62, 68
Titov, 61
Trengrouse, Henry, 16
Tsiolkovsky, Konstantine, 20, 21, *67*

U.S.S.R., 45, 64, 65
United Kingdom, 57
United States, *see* America
Uranus, *91*
V-2 rocket, 28, 32, *33,* 34, 37, 50,
Van Allen, James, 47
Valier, Max, 18, 19
Vanguard rocket, 35, 36, 39, 50, 51
Venus, 52, 53, 76, 77, 88, 90, *91*
   space probe, 53

Verne, Jules, 20
Veronique rocket, 35
Viking rocket, 33, 34, 35, 36, 51
Viper rocket, *40*
Von Braun, Wernher, 32
Vostock spacecraft, *46,* 58, 59, 60, 61

Wac Corporal missile, 32, 34
Wan Hu, 20
Waterloo, 14
White, Edward, 62
White Sands, (New Mexico, U.S.), 32
World War I, 16
World War II, 16, 40, 50, 82, 85
   D-Day, 14

X-1 & *X-1A* (Bell), 40, 41
X-15 (Bell), 25, 42, 43
X-20 (Bell), 44
XB-64, 82
XSM-64, 83
Yegorov, Boris, 61
Young, John, 62, 63
Zeppelins, 16

Figures in italic refer to illustrations